# A Beginner's Guide to Bee Farming

by

Daniel Brett Runkle
M.Div, M.S.E.S

**BLACK & WHITE FIELD MANUAL EDITION**

Promised Land Bee Farm Publishing

Fort Worth                    2017                    Texas

**Promised Land Bee Farm Publishing**
4129 County Road 920, Crowley, TX 76036, USA

———————————————

© Daniel B. Runkle 2017
B&W Field Manual Edition

Cover Photo by Sarah Hodson
Photos by Sarah Hodson & Daniel Runkle
Queen Cell Photo on Page 88 by Mike Bright

ISBN-13: 978-1981439263
ISBN-10: 1981439269



**PRINTED IN THE UNITED STATES OF AMERICA**

# Forward

 In the late Summer of 2009 we had just returned from a visit to our friends in the South Bay area of Los Angeles, CA, where my wife and I had first met and been married.  One Saturday morning we were enjoying a jar of Orange blossom honey from our CA visit, and I mentioned beekeeping.  My wife replied, you should get back into it, and remarked how neat it would be to harvest our own honey.  There at the breakfast table I prayed, Lord, if it's in your will please help me to get back into beekeeping.

That same Saturday we'd already planned to travel up to Wise county to look for land, but returned home discouraged from the location.  Later that day I chanced to walk around the back of the house.  There on the Southeast corner of our house, on a fig tree branch, was a small swarm.  This was the first swarm of bees I had seen in over 25 years, and felt that it was a sovereign confirmation of the Lord's direction to return to beekeeping.  (A photo of that swarm can be seen on page 116.)

Daniel B. Runkle

# Contents

# Introduction

## So You Want to Be a Beekeeper?

When I was about fourteen years old, living in Tampa, Florida, I enrolled in an elective Agriculture class at Buchanan Jr. High School.  In addition to an interest in raising rabbits, one of the things that caught my eye was a booklet on beekeeping.  This was a hobby that I'd seen my great Uncle Ennis pursue at his farm in Quincy, Florida.  At about the same time, I rejoined Boy Scouts and discovered the Beekeeper's Merit Badge. With so many resources at my disposal, I was soon well on my way to becoming a beekeeper.

After reading the booklet on Beekeeping, I went to the library at Buchanan Jr. High, and found a two inch thick, embossed and gilded volume of the "ABC and XYZ of Bee Culture" from the A.I. Root Bee Library which was printed in 1947.  It was 1974 and I felt like I was opening an ancient treasure chest of beekeeping knowledge from the past.  On my family's trip to the North Florida panhandle that Thanksgiving, I devoured the entire book, approximately 720 pages.

**Figure 1: Root's Original ABC and XYZ Manual**

While visiting my grandfather and grandmother, my next stop was my Uncle Ennis' farm near Quincy.  He walked me out to his small apiary, along with my grandfather, my dad, my cousin,

and my brother.  I'll never forget the experience of watching
my 65-year-old grandfather quickly race away from the
colonies as he was pursued by one of Uncle Ennis's bees.  It
seems that the bees had a particular affinity for Vitalis hair
tonic.  I was not deterred by the bee chasing experience; in
fact, while reading about beekeeping in that Root tome, I
became intrigued by the thought of delving into a colony of
more than 50,000 bees, while encapsulated inside the
protective screens and fabrics of my bee suit.

Outside the protection of that bee suit it would only take 150
stings to kill a person.  As a 14 year old boy in 1974, I was
living in Florida where the Apollo space program was in full
steam.  This was the early trailblazing days of the astronauts
working inside their protective space suits.  So, this protective
layering of the bee suit seemed like a thrilling parallel to the
astronaut.  Although the threat of death by stings was a bit
intimidating, the hobby seemed like a pretty cool adventure
to a 14 year old in 1974.

After doing a good bit of reading in Root's ABC & XYZ
reference book, I began my search for bees.  At first I tried to
see if I could triangulate the location of a nearby colony by
capturing a bee and watching his flight path after release.
However, this didn't work well.  After a series of failed search
missions, a neighbor's dad, who worked as welder in the
Tampa Bay shipyard, informed me of a colony of bees he had
seen in a section of pipe at the shipyard.

About the same time, I contacted one of the BSA's merit
badge counselors about working on the Beekeeping merit
badge.  Using a frame of brood he had given me, and with a
good bit of experienced coaching from him, I was able to trap
out the swarm of bees from the pipe and into a Langstroth
type hive that I had built.  This is a brief introduction to my

early beginnings of becoming a beekeeper, and the small beekeeping business that I was soon to name "Brett's Bees."

Note: The idea for the name came along about 1978, by which time I was producing enough honey to sell, and should be attributed to my mother's boss at the time, Mrs. Coaker.

In this handbook I've tried to include all the basic essentials that a person would need to know to get started in beekeeping.  You can study bees and beekeeping for a lifetime, but this text should be able to help you to get started in one of the most amazing forms of farming that a person can learn.

# Chapter 1

## Equipment Basics

The first thing one needs to begin beekeeping is the proper equipment. This includes the protective clothing, smoker, hive tools, and hive setup itself. There are a variety of other tools, clothing, specialized hive parts, extracting equipment, and other bee paraphernalia which can be purchased, but these are the rudiments for getting started. In this chapter these basic essentials will be covered.

### 1. Protective Clothing.

**a. Veil.** Probably one of the most important pieces of equipment that a beekeeper can own is the beekeeper's veil. A beginning beekeeper should never attempt to open a colony of bees without a veil. Although more experienced beekeepers at times will attempt to check and manipulate colonies without a veil, this is strictly according to the temperament of the colony and should never be attempted by a beginner. Even the experienced beekeeper will

**Figure 2: Detached Screen Veil & Hat**

have a veil and gloves handy nearby in case a colony becomes defensive or agitated.

When donning a veil, remember to make sure it is well-secured by tie downs or Velcro with no gaps or openings where bees could intrude into the face and neck area. An aggressive colony can quickly find an unsecured opening and can fill the inside of your veil

**Figure 3: Integrated Veil & Jacket**

and face area with 15 to 20 angry bees within seconds. If you find that the colony you are working has become overly aggressive, it is wise to consult a more experienced beekeeper from your local beekeeper's association. See chapter 9 section 6 for more information on dealing with Africanized honeybees.

There are a variety of veil options that can be found in a beekeeper's supply catalog. For a stand-alone veil you can use a square folding screen veil with a vented mesh helmet (as shown in Figure 2). You could also use a round veil with a vented helmet, or a veil with a built in cloth hat.

Another option that many beekeepers use, which is a bit more costly, is a veil that is integrated with a white

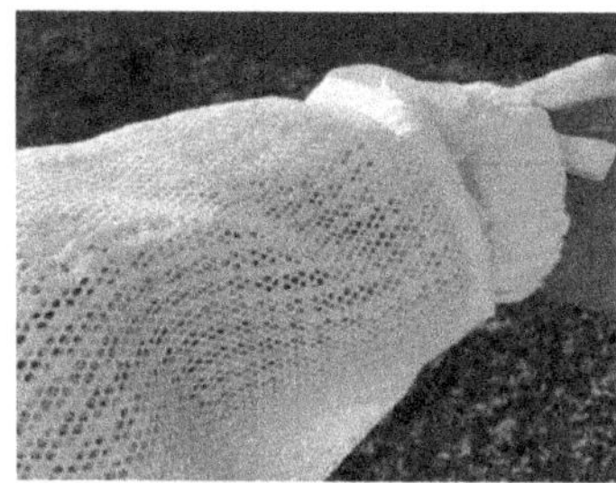

**Figure 5: Screen Mesh**

beekeeper's jacket, shown in Figure 3  These are

**Figure 4: Vented Mesh Jacket**

zipped and Velcroed onto the jacket, and are one of the more convenient options.

A slight variation on the jacket with the integrated veil is the vented jacket and veil (shown in Figure 4).  This vented jacket is made of an outer fine screened mesh with an underlying course mesh as shown in Figure 5. This course mesh helps keep the lighter mesh off the skin and thus prevents bee stings from penetrating underlying skin.

The other option is the full beekeeper's suit with

**Figure 6: Full Bee Suit with Integrated Veil**

integrated veil (See Figure 6).  The full bee suit is probably the most practical option for the beginning beekeeper that is learning how to handle bees.  This can ordered as a cotton fabric, or as screen mesh as shown in Figure 5.

Whatever the choice of veil, it is always important for the beekeeper to wear the traditional white suit on the upper body.  This is due to the fact that darker colors, especially black, can induce an aggressive response by the bees.  White has been shown over the centuries to have a calming influence on bee behavior.

**b. Gloves.**  Like the other areas of protective clothing, bee supply houses provide a number of options to choose from in addition to the basic gloves.  Aside from the size of your gloves, the primary option is glove material.

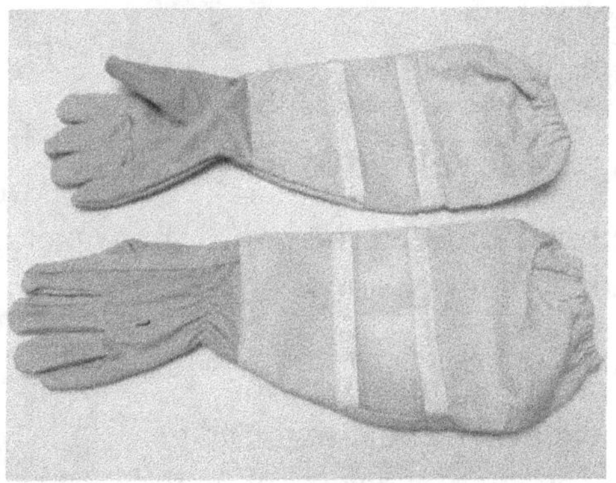

**Figure 7: Soft Leather Gloves with Vent**

When I first started in the 70's, I used the basic thick cotton gloves with the elastically drawn cuffs which extend almost to the elbows that came with my basic beekeeper's kit.  However, I soon discovered that bees can often sting through these cloth gloves.  So, I promptly switched over to soft cow leather gloves, with a screen vented cuff, and cotton sleeves.  I've used these ever since.

Another glove that has since become available is the same vented arrangement of the glove of my second choice, but with a softer, goat leather over the hands.  This can provide a little more "feel" to the glove when handling the bees.

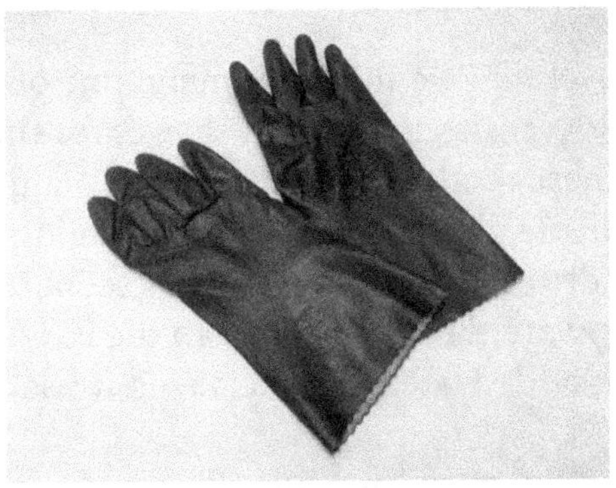

**Figure 8: Nitrile Gloves**

The other few options which have come available in the last few decades are plastic coated cotton gloves and reusable Nitrile gloves. The puncture resistant Nitrile gloves are usually adhesively coated over a cotton liner.  These are particularly useful when working with bee medications, or when doing beekeeping operations that involve a lot of uncapped or cut honey.  They can be really helpful for the advanced beekeeper doing cut-outs or bee removals which involve the removal of honeycomb, brood & honey, since it's easier to clean honey off of the Nitrile than

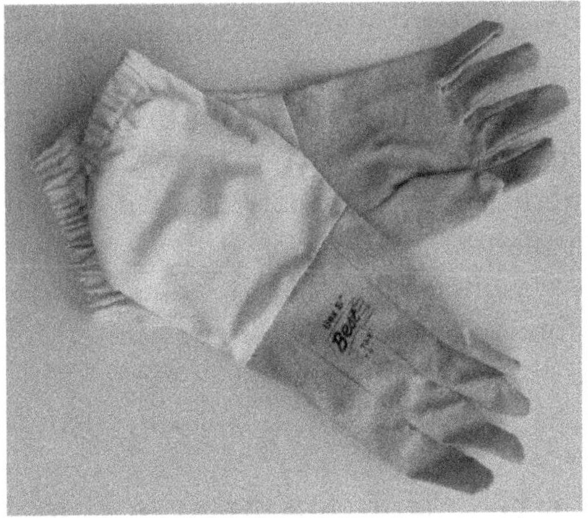

**Figure 9: Coated Cotton Gloves**

leather.  The downside of the Nitrile gloves is that they are fluid resistant, and do not breathe.  For that reason they get quite hot and sweaty inside.

Overall, I would recommend one of the basic soft leather gloves with the vented sleeves for the beginning beekeeper. These cost a bit more than the plain cotton, plastic coated or Nitrile gloves, but the comfort and protection make them well worth the investment.  They seem to breathe and vent better and are therefore cooler to the hands. The other options can be added later for specialized work.

**c. Jacket or Suit.**  As a beginner beekeeper, I utilized a zippered white cotton painter's coverall's, which worked well for a time.  It is particularly important to use a zippered version, since the bees will crawl in between buttons. However, this full cotton suit seemed to be a bit hot at times.

Most beekeeping supply houses offer both jackets and suits which often have integrated bee veils. Although a beginner may be more comfortable in a full-body suit, a more experienced beekeeper may opt for the jacket and veil. Which form you choose, whether jacket or suit, is typically dependent on the disposition of your bees.  I usually wear jeans with the jacket option, and tuck the cuffs of my pants into my thick socks if wearing tennis shoes.  However, another option for footwear is to wear rubber boots, and tuck the pants into the boot.  This is usually sufficient to keeps the bees from crawling up the pants and stinging the legs.  The rubber boots also seem to be a deterrent against pesky redbugs, which seem to like the tall grass fields that are usually associated with beehive locations.

One of the big factors in suit choice is not always how hot the weather is, but how "hot" the bees are.  For the more aggressive, or "hot" colony, a full suit is definitely advisable. More recently some of the supply houses have offered a version of the original Golden Bee's vented suits and jackets that have been shown to perform well with Africanized colonies.

As mentioned under integrated veils, the vented suit uses a fine screen mesh on the outside, lifted by a more course rubbery mesh on the inside.  This keeps the fine mesh spaced away from your body, and at the same time allows a reasonable amount of cool ventilation for the beekeeper.  This is probably one of the more expensive and luxurious versions of bee suits.  The one disadvantage is that it does not work well in areas where there are briars or thorns that can tear the delicate outer mesh.

For the beginning beekeeper, I would recommend the zippered light cotton bee suit with veil.  A vented jacket and veil can be used later once the beekeeper becomes better accustomed to stings, and better at judging the temperament of his or her colony.

**2. Smoker.**  The smoker is a tool that you never want to do without.  The Lord has designed bees with a unique instinct to protect their colonies in case of natural disasters, such as forest fires.  The smoke from the smoker induces the bees to begin gorging themselves with honey, in preparation for a mass

**Figure 10: Basic Smoker**

exodus or swarm in case their home is burning down.  When they're full of honey, they're happy and much less likely to sting.  However, one must beware of over-smoking, which can lead to swarming behavior, and the loss of your colony.

Like other equipment, there are a variety of smokers which can be purchased from bee supply companies. Most beekeepers choose a stainless steel smoker so that the smoker will stand up to corrosion and wear.  Another important feature to have is an integrated wire cage to protect both the beekeeper and the environment from the very hot sides of the smoker.  It's important for the beekeeper always to be careful about where he sets the hot smoker, so that the very hot bottom does not ignite dry grass, leaves, or other flammable materials.

Professional beekeepers sometimes opt for the 10-inch-high smokers in order to hold a larger capacity of smoker fuel.  However, as long as you're not going to be working scores of beehives in one day, the 7-inch-high smoker should suffice for the beginner and even the sideline beekeeper.

You don't need to purchase smoker fuel from the beekeeping supply companies.  This is an unnecessarily expensive way of doing things.  Common materials that have been used by keepers include: pine shavings, pine needles, cedar shavings, strips of cotton clothing, Spanish moss, and burlap.  These are all items that can either be acquired by scrap or by a relatively inexpensive purchase at the local feed store.  All these materials can be effectively used to provide a nice smoke to calm the bees.

**Figure 11: Various Hive Tools**

**3. Hive Tools.** There are several key tools in beekeeping that are generally referred to as "hive tools." They include the basic hive tool itself, which is typically a 10" long tapered metal piece with a flange on the end for prying up frames. The hive tool is used for separating hive boxes by prying between boxes which have been sealed by propolis, or bee glue. If you ever leave this item at home, you'll soon learn how important this tool is. It's also used to pry up the frames which are likewise glued together by propolis. Another version of the frame tool is referred to as the "frame lifter." This has a "J" shape on the end where the flange is, and is inserted down and underneath the ears of the frame, which can be pried up by leverage. The J-shape acts as a finger to get under the frame end, and the heel acts as a prying fulcrum. This is a tool that I myself prefer over the

12

traditional hive tool.  The J end can also be used to pull out entrance reducers when switching back and forth from summer to winter hive opening sizes.

**4.  Hive.**  Another one of the most essential items in beekeeping is the hive itself.  The most common hive that's

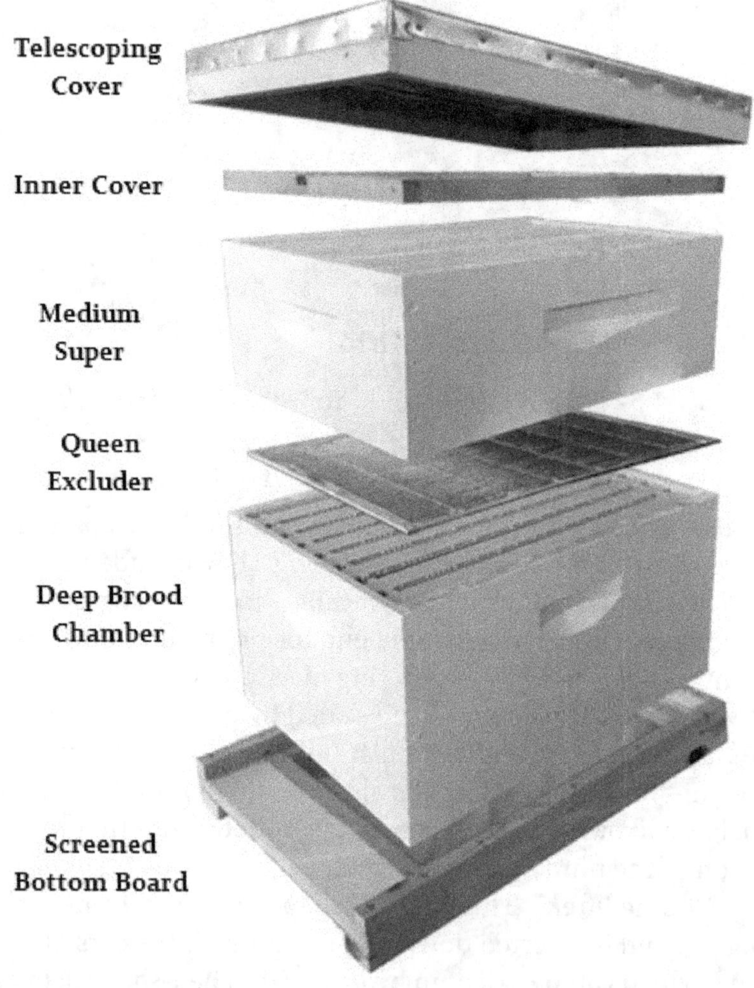


**Figure 12: Langstroth Hive Components**

used in the United States is the Langstroth Hive, as shown in Figure 12 on the previous page.   The typical hive includes a top cover, honey super, brood chamber, bottom board and entrance reducer.

a. **Top Cover**.  There are several options which can be used for a top cover.  Probably the most common cover is the telescoping cover with inner cover. (See Langstroth exploded view in Figure 12.)  This design provides a 3/8 inch space above the inner cover for bees to crawl up into and it provides protected ventilation via a 3/4-inch slot in the inner cover. The cover itself has a lip or flange that extends down over the sides of the underlying super or brood-chamber and these covers are usually topped with a sheet of tin, copper, or aluminum to protect the colony from rain.

A slightly more economical cover that is used by the commercial beekeeper is the migratory cover.  This cover is

**Figure 13: Homemade Migratory Cover w/ Feeder Port**

usually a solid 3/4-inch wooden cover with flanges on the front and back, but with no inner cover, and no side flange. This allows commercial beekeepers to closely stack colonies side by side.  A homemade version of the cover with a 16 oz small bottle feeding port is shown in Figure 13. These covers are usually around half the cost of a telescoping hive and are more convenient than telescoping covers for bundling colonies for shipping.

**b. Super**. The top story in a hive is usually referred to as the honey super.  This is the area of the colony where the honey stores are kept.  There are deep supers which hold 9-5/8" deep frames, medium supers which hold 6-5/8" medium frames, and shallow supers which contain 5-3/4" shallow frames.  As honey is produced, additional supers can be added on top of the first super.

**Figure 14: Medium Depth Super (8 Frame Shown)**

Most beekeepers are no longer using the shallow frames and supers, but are typically usually using the medium depth frames for honey supers.  Commercial beekeepers typically use only deep supers.

One advantage of using the medium supers are that they are a reasonable height which to be quickly and fully drawn out and filled with honey by the bees, while a deeper super requires a more robust flow of honey for the bees to draw out and fill.  The other advantage is that the medium supers are lighter and, therefore can be individually handled more easily than deeper supers.

**c. Brood Chamber.** The brood chamber is usually the lowest portion of the colony's stack of supers or hive bodies. This is the reproductive engine for the colony, where the queen bee lays her eggs, which are then nurtured from larvae to form pupae and finally adult bees.

The brood chamber can either be made up of one or two deep supers, or two or three medium supers. In more recent years,

**Figure 15: 9-5/8" Deep Hive Body (8 Frame)**

some beekeepers have gone to using medium depth hive bodies for both brood chamber and honey supers. This adds the convenience of interchangeability of frames for hive splits. (Hive splits are another way of reproducing a new colony which will be studied later.)

**d. Queen Excluder.**  One component of the hive which is often used by beekeepers to keep brood from being laid in the honey supers is called a queen excluder.  This is a wire mesh, or plastic mesh barrier that is placed between the supers above and the brood chamber below.  This barrier allows the

**Figure 16: Queen Excluder (8 Frame Shown)**

worker bees to pass through freely, but the spacing of the wires, or plastic slots will not allow the larger bodied queen to pass through.   In this way the queen is "excluded" from the honey stores.  Drones are also excluded from the honey stores above.

Some beekeepers do not find the queen excluder necessary, being careful to remove only honey frames for extraction.  However, even the most experienced beekeeper can sometimes miss seeing patches of brood and pollen that have been placed among the stores of honey.  This can result in brood being opened and destroyed during honey uncapping and extraction if you're not careful.

The beginner beekeeper should use the queen excluder for keeping brood areas and honey areas separate.  However, it's important to remember that the queen excluder must be removed before winter sets in.  This is because the winter bee cluster will move about the hive boxes as it uses up the stores of honey in the vicinity of the cluster.  If the queen is excluded from the area of the colony that has the honey stores and the cluster, the queen could become isolated in the cold and die. This would leave a colony unable to reproduce, and the entire colony would subsequently die.

**e. Entrance Reducer.**  Another important part of the hive architecture is the entrance reducer.  This is usually a ¾ in by ¾ in piece of wood that spans the length of the entrance at

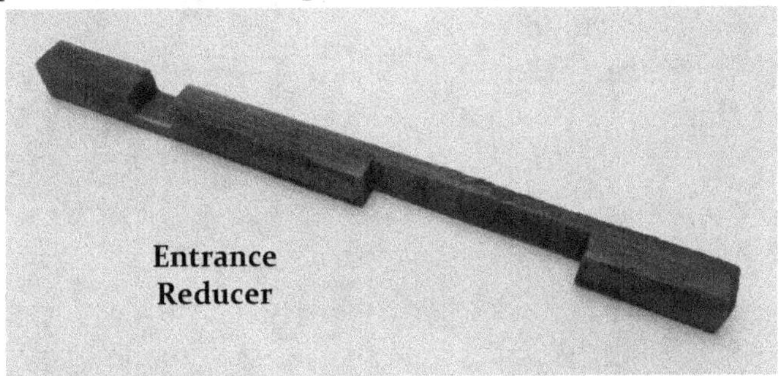


**Figure 17: Entrance Reducer (8 Frame Shown)**

the bottom board's opening.  The reducer usually has a 4 in wide in by 7/16 in high large slot for summer access, and a 5/8 in wide in by 7/16 in high smaller slot for a winter bee access. During honey flows the entire entrance reducer can be removed allowing for a large influx of bees into the colony.

Since the colony has guard bees posted at the entrance of a hive, it's important to keep weaker colonies protected with a smaller entrance setting.  This prevents robbing by other stronger colonies who may attempt to overwhelm the guard bees at the entrance of the colony. Reducers also help guard bees manage the entrance from intruders such as wasps, wax moths, and hive beetles. The setting of the size of the entrance is accomplished by rotating the entrance reducer by 90 degrees.

There are other specialized metal entrance reducers that can be purchased from bee supply houses.  These can be designed in a variety of ways, either to keep the queen from exiting the colony or to keep mice from entering the wooden openings and nesting inside the colony during the winter, while the colony is somewhat dormant in a winter cluster.

**e.  Bottom Board.**  In bygone years, bottom boards were relatively simple.  These usually were made from a solid piece of pine, or cypress and had ¾ in by ¾ in supports that ran around three sides of the bottom end of the

**Figure 18: Solid Bottom Board (8 Frame)**

**Figure 19: Screened Varroa Bottom Board (8 Frame)**

brood chamber box.  This provided a ¾ in opening along one of the short ends of the brood chamber.

Today's beekeeper is faced with a variety of scourges including varroa mites, hive beetles, tracheal mites, and wax moths.  One of the recent innovations to help reduce the varroa mite population in a colony is to provide a screened bottom board.  This allows the beekeeper to treat the colony with a dousing of powdered sugar, which will usually help dislodge varroa mites from the backs of the bees.  The varroa mites then drop to the bottom board, but instead of crawling back up the sides of the colony, they fall to the ground and die.

Screened bottom boards are a part of pest management referred to as Integrated Pest Management (IPM). Using a variety of IPM tools helps to significantly reduce the varroa mite population in a colony, by slowing down the varroa reproductive cycle in a holistic manner.

**f. Feeder**. Another important item to include in the basic architecture of your hive is the feeder.  Here again there are a number of possible options.  One of the older and simpler feeders is the **Boardman feeder**.  This is made with an inverted quart jar of sugar syrup, which sits in wooden block at the entrance of the hive. The lid has multiple small 1/32 in holes, similar to a

**Figure 20: Boardman Feeder**

watering can head.  The tiny holes allow bees to feed from underneath the inverted jar.

This feeder has an opening toward the inside of the hive, as it slips into the entrance, and cantilevers off the front landing board of the colony.  Unfortunately, this means of feeding is the most prone to attracting other nearby bees, who with relative ease fight their way into the feeder, since the feeder is located at the entrance of the colony.  This ends up oftentimes inducing a robbing frenzy by other stronger colonies.

**Figure 21: Top Feeder (8 Frame)**

One option less prone to robbing is the **top feeder**.  These feeders are usually constructed like a shallow super, but instead of frames, these feeders usually have two large compartments into which the sugar syrup is poured, and stored. Bees enter from beneath the feeder up through a slot that is provided in the middle of the feeder, and crawl over the side and down to the feed. The compartments usually have wooden or plastic "floats", which enable the bees to access the surface of the syrup without drowning. Bees attempting to rob a top feeder would have to make it through the entire colony of bees to access the top feeder. Consequently, this feeder is one of the better options.

There is also a **homemade top feeder** which is somewhat of a hybrid of the first two options. This can be created using a ½ in or ¾ in plywood that is sized to the width and length of the brood chamber or super. This board is then drilled with one or two 2 ½ in holes. These holes allow inverted feeder jars to be placed above the colony. Some beekeepers actually drill the hole in the migratory cover. This also allows the beekeeper to monitor the consumption of the sugar syrup.

**Figure 22: Homemade Top Feeder (8 Frame)**

An empty super is then placed over the plywood cover with the inverted sugar syrup, and the top cover is placed over that super. This method has the advantage of keeping the syrup at a warmer temperature, rather than having the jars exposed to the cold outdoor temperatures during fall or winter.

The other feeder that is commonly used is the **frame feeder** (see Figure 23). This is typically manufactured out of plastic, is often about the width of a frame, and is lowered into the brood chamber next to the adjacent frames. Although it usually takes up the width of at least one frame, some variants are actually as wide as two frames.

One of the downsides of the frame feeder is the tendency for bees to end up drowning in the syrup. This can be prevented by providing some type of float on the surface of the syrup. I've found that a typical paint stirrer is about the right thickness and width to provide a helpful float for the bees. When I've used this float method, I've seen that the number of drowned bees ending up in the bottom of the feeder has been dramatically reduced, if not eliminated.

**Figure 23: Frame Feeder (8 Frame)**

# Chapter 2

## Basic Bee Life and Nomenclature

**1. Bee Types & Roles**.  There are three basic types of bees in a colony – the Queen, the Worker and the Drone.  Each of the three types of bees has a different set of roles within the life of the colony.

**a.  Queen** -  The Queen bee is a female bee who has the most central role of the entire colony.  Her role is to be the primary reproductive source of progeny to the colony.  She is also thought to be involved in the decision making of the colony as to where the colony will live, how it will get there, and how long she will remain. This is debated though, and some consider the scout bees to be more essential keys in the decision making process of selecting a new home to the colony.

**Figure 24: Queen with Workers**

Nevertheless, wherever the queen ends up going, the other bees will faithfully follow her pheromone scent.

Shown below is a queen surrounded by her attending worker bees, and nurse bees. The queen bee is the largest of the three types of bees.  She possesses an elongated abdomen which has uniquely developed as a result of a steady diet of royal jelly during the larval stage of development.  Although the queen bee does not have eyes as big as a drone, she does have eyes that are larger than the worker.  Her wings and legs are likewise much larger than both the worker and the drone.

The primary role of the queen is egg laying.  Depending on the nectar flow and the environmental conditions, the queen will lay as many as 5,000 eggs per day.  Considering the fact that an average colony may have approximately 50-60,000 bees, this demonstrates how quickly a colony population can be built up. The queen will increase her egg laying when there are sufficient pollen stores and nectar flow, and will decrease her laying during times of drought, or severely cold weather. A good laying queen will lay a nice full pattern of brood, and will do so at climate-appropriate times.

In the early days of the queen, the virgin queen will emerge from her peanut shaped queen cell and shortly after take flight for her initial mating flight.  Once she takes flight, nearby drones will follow her with the hopes of mating with the newly emerged queen.  The queen can mate with as many as three to four different drones, and will carry the fertilizing sperm in a specialized pouch for the rest of her life.

**b. Worker** - The worker bee is a female bee which is tasked with the most essential and basic roles within the colony. Although the worker bee is not capable of reproduction within the colony, she is instrumental in almost all of the essential tasks within the colony.

The worker bee is identified as the smallest of the three types of bees.  The bee that you most often see in the field is the female worker bee.  She has smaller eyes, smaller abdomen, smaller thorax and smaller legs than the Queen and the Drone.   However her wings are about the same size as the queen.

In the early days of a worker, it initially acts as a nurse bee. These adolescent bees are usually identified by their smaller and fuzzier appearance than that of the older adult bees.  The nurse bees produce a substance referred to as Royal Jelly which is fed to the queen bee larvae.  Additionally, they also produce the lesser, more honey-like version of royal jelly that is fed to developing worker and drone larvae.

As the nurse bees become older, they begin to take part in the hunting and gathering function of the colony.  It's during this time that the worker bees begin to forage for nectar and pollen from the surrounding flowers. Thousands of bees are involved in this very important role in the life of the colony.

Another role that the adult bees have is in the area of wax production. During a strong flow of honey, bees will be storing and consuming larger quantities of nectar.  Whereas humans produce fat when we eat excessive amounts of food, bees produce wax, which is conveniently extruded in scales on the lower abdomen area of the worker bee. This is then used to build the honeycomb cells which function both as compartments for egg, larva, and pupa development, as well as being used for nectar and pollen storage.

As the worker bees become older, they can also serve as guard bees at the entrance area of the colony.  These guards station themselves at the entrance and inspect the incoming bees for the appropriate and familiar pheromone of the queen.  If an incoming bee bears the pheromone of another colony, the guard bee will begin biting at the wings and body parts of the intruding bee, and begin working with another guard bee to drag the intruder away from the entrance to the colony.

Guard behavior is also exhibited by the worker bees against humans, animals, birds or predatory insects that come too close to the entrance of the colony.  Since a worker will lose her life if she stings a creature, bees will sometimes exhibit a head butting behavior to warn off intruders.  If you experience a bee bumping against your body or face, this is their way of telling you to "get out of our territory".

**b.  Drone** - The drone bee is a male bee whose primary task is reproduction.  The drone is identified as the second largest of the three types of bees.  Drones have larger eyes, larger abdomen  diameter, and larger thorax when compared to both workers and queens.  However, the legs of the drones are about the same size as those of the queen, which are larger

**Figure 25: Drone with Workers**

27

than those of the worker.

There are hundreds of drones that are produced in a typical colony, compared to the thousands of worker bees that are produced.  Drone cells are much larger, being wider in diameter, and longer in depth, and for this reason are usually laid around the perimeter of frames/combs.

Genetically, a drone is produced by an unfertilized egg.  The queen has the ability to control whether she lays a drone egg, or a worker's fertilized egg.  The queen is generally responding to the size of the wax cell that she is laying in.  A worker brood cell will be a smaller honeycomb cell size, which is more typical, while the drone cell is enlarged in both diameter and length.  In a frame of both drone and worker brood, you will notice the capped drone cells standing out taller and puffier on the comb surface.  Worker brood is puffier than capped honey, but both brood cappings will have a more flat light brown papery appearance than the wax honey cappings.  This is because the brood cappings are porous for oxygen exchange, while capped honey has a wax seal.

There is a tendency to view the drone as a less than useful member of the bee community, since his roles appear to be relegated to eating and reproduction.  This is in contrast to the worker bee who is involved in early nursing duties, and eventually tasked with bringing pollen and nectar back to the colony.  However, the drone does play an important role of being the carrier and provider of the genetic material necessary for the reproduction of the entire colony.

Only a handful of drones will be involved in providing that lifelong genetic material to the Queen during her once in a lifetime mating flight.  Yet when the mating flight is over, the drone ends up falling back to earth eviscerated as a result of his sacrificial contribution to the life of the colony. Drones are also killed off during fall and dearth periods for the colony, in order to reduce honey consumption.

**2. Basic Bee Anatomy**. There are five basic constituent parts to a bee's anatomy the head, thorax, abdomen, legs and wings (See Figures 26 & 27). The drone bee has the largest head and eyes, with the queen bee following in close second, and the worker having the smallest head. In all genders, bees have compound eyes, each of which is composed of hundreds of tiny lenses. This compound vision is especially helpful in discerning subtleties of depth and color which provide the bee with an ability to navigate the fields of flowers for pollen and nectar.

It is claimed among many scientific journals that bees are unable to see red, and can only see the lower frequency wavelengths of reflected light. However, this doesn't appear to deter them from being attracted to, or finding flowers that are red.

Bees have two pairs of wings, the forewing and hind wing attached on each side of the upper and outermost thorax. These two forward and aft wings are actually attached to one another by a line of hook-like devices that connect the forward and aft wings together, forming a unified linked lifting surface. (See Figure 26) These hooks are called the forward and aft hamuli. The wings themselves are made up of a number of cells, linked and supported by veins running between the cells for structural strength

# Basic Bee Wing Anatomy

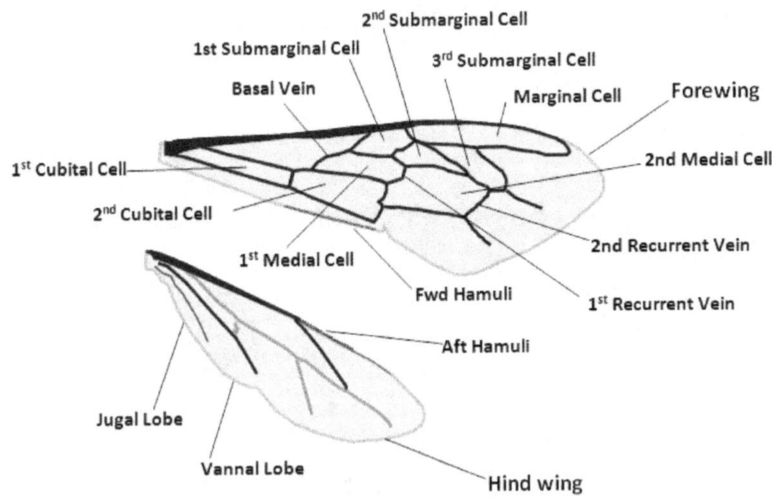


**Figure 26: Wing Anatomy & Parts**

One key health indicator for a colony is the appearance of the bee's wings. If bees at the entrance or inside of a colony appear to have small or disfigured wings, this can indicate that the colony is suffering from a Varroa mite infestation. Varroa mites often carry a virus which leads to wing deformity in juvenile bees. The presence of deformed wings is an indication that treatment for mites may be needed.

Examining the bee's upper thorax is another way to discern the health of your colony.  A fuzzy thorax indicates a juvenile bee.  The more mature worker bee will often be seen to have the fuzz balding or rubbed off due to age and wear.  This thorax area is a location upon which varroa mites will often attach themselves.  Varroa mites can appear like a tiny seed attached to the thorax or back of the bee.

## Basic Bee Anatomy

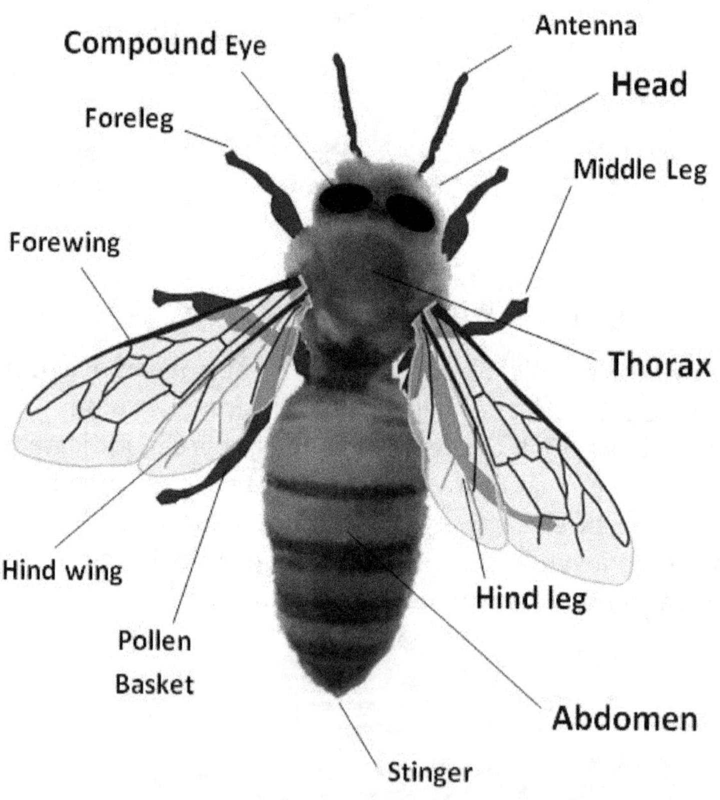


**Figure 27: Anatomical Parts of Honeybee**

The underside of the abdomen is the location where wax scales are extruded.  Many people are very familiar with the aft most portion of the bee's abdomen.  This is where the stinger is located.  Unfortunately, when a bee stings an adversary, the stinger is torn from the bee's abdomen along with a venom sack.  This soon leads to the death of the brave bee protecting her colony.  However, the single bee has now "tagged" its adversary with the venom and bee pheromone. This venom smell will now lead to defensive behavior by other nearby bees as well, ultimately aiding in the defense of the nearby colony.  For this reason, if you're in the bee yard with no protective equipment and you're stung, it's important to either don protective gear or move away from the colonies as soon as possible. Bear in mind that, once you have been stung, you are now carrying a written chemical invitation for more stings.

## 3. Basic Bee Development

There are three developing phases of a bee, the egg stage, the larval stage and the pupa stage. The figure below shows an egg in the bottom of a honeycomb cell. One of the best ways to check for

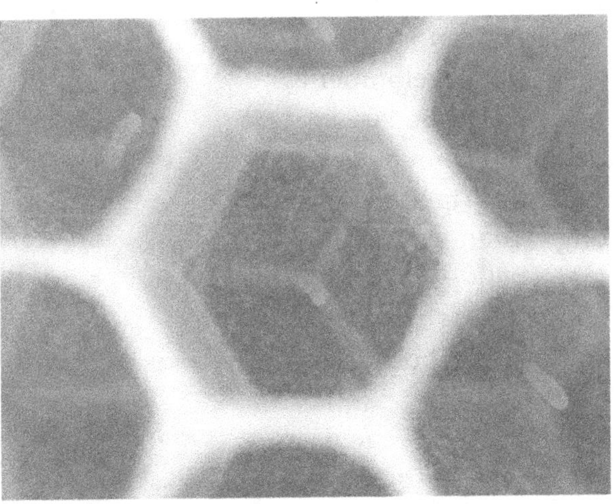

**Figure 28: Egg in Honeycomb Cell**

eggs in a frame is to hold the frame up, with the sun to your back. This will help illuminate the tiny eggs inside the bottom of the cell. These cells can usually be found around the perimeter of brood cells that are hatching out, or inside a hatched out area, in which the queen has subsequently laid eggs .

The egg stage of development appears like a tiny grain of rice in the bottom of a cell. On the third day after laying, the egg hatches into the larval stage. In their early life, the larvae are fed a milky white substance, which is similar in consistency to royal jelly. Female eggs being groomed for the role as queen are fed copious amounts of royal jelly, and are raised in the larger compartment of the queen cell.

The next phase of development is the larval stage. There are two phases of the larval stage, the uncapped phase and the capped phase. In the first uncapped phase, both female queens and workers remain uncapped in days 4-8 of the development process. Drone larvae are uncapped from days 4-10, remaining open 2 days longer than worker and queen cells. In addition to being larger than the worker bees, both the longer open time and larger cell make the drone a more vulnerable target for Varroa mite intrusion.

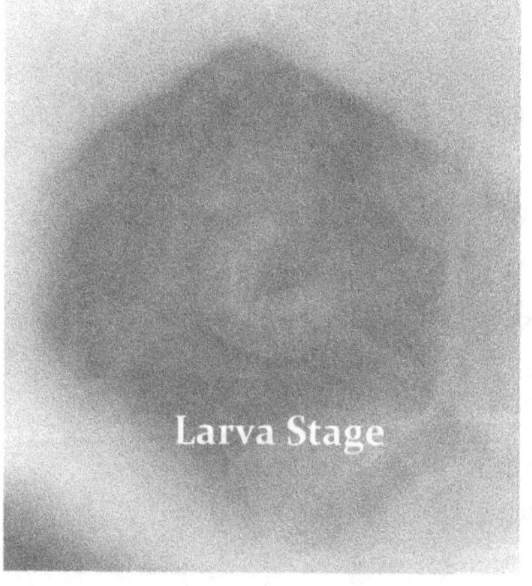


**Figure 29: Larva in Honeycomb Cell**

The capped larval phase lasts from days 9-13 for the worker bee, and 9-12 for the queen bee.  Drones require more time than queens and workers in the capped larval phase, abiding in this phase from days 11-17.  So, this means that a queen takes 12 days before reaching pupa.  A worker takes 13 days before reaching the pupa stage, and the drone takes a full 17 days from laid egg to pupa.

The final pupal phase is surprisingly short when compared to the larval stage. Queens emerge on day 16, after developing 3 days as a pupa.  Workers emerge on day 21 after developing 7 days as a pupa.  Drones emerge on day 24, after having spent 6 days in the pupa phase.  The adjacent figure shows a close-up photograph of a drone pupa.

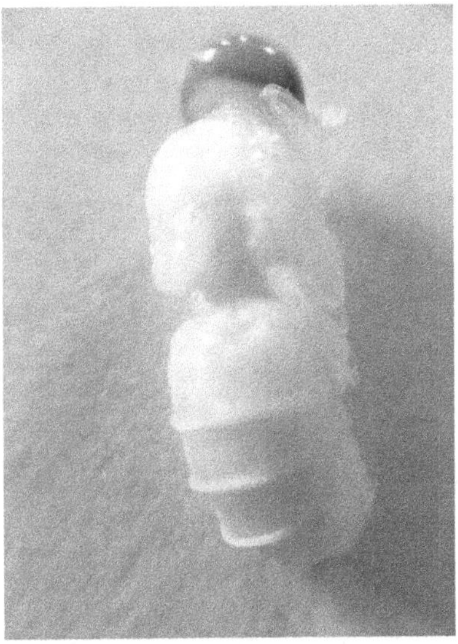

**Figure 30: Drone Pupal Stage**

As young bees hatch out from their porous capped cells, nurse bees feed the hungry newborns as they extend their hungry tongues through the capped cell as it is chewed away.

# Chapter 3

## Simple Ways to Acquire the Colony

There are five basic ways of acquiring a colony that are reasonable means for a beginning beekeeper:  ordering package bees, ordering a nuclear colony, buying a full hive, collecting a swarm, or trapping out a colony.

### 1.  Ordering Package Bees.

Some think that ordering package bees is the simplest way to acquire bees.  This can be done through the United States Mail, and usually includes 3 pounds of bees, a queen bee in a queen cage, and a quart can of sugar syrup for feeding the bees in transit.

There are a variety of companies that offer packaged bees, which can be picked up from the supplier or shipped by mail. It is important to make sure that the home for your bees is prepared and ready before the bees are shipped to your location.

Once the bees have arrived and your full hive with frames is set up in an appropriate location (see section on Locating Your Hive), you're ready to introduce your bees to their new home.  How you go about this can mean the difference between success and failure.  Many experienced beekeepers have ordered package bees only to lose them shortly thereafter when they take to the sky and swarm.

One method of introducing the swarm to the new home is to place the caged queen between two frames in the middle of

**Figure 31: Placement of Queen Cage for Release**

the hive body (See above Figure).  Sometimes a bent paperclip carefully passed through the holes of the plastic cage is helpful in suspending the cage from the top frames.  This keeps the cage from dropping to the bottom of the brood chamber.  The new plastic queen cages have a plastic tubular section that is filled with candy fondant, while the old wooden cages have fondant filling one of the three circular end compartments. When you place the cage, it's important to ensure that the cork or stopper on the end with the fondant is removed so that there is a timed release of the queen to her colony.  The bees will be drawn to the queen's cage and will gradually remove the fondant candy from her blocked passage, releasing the queen to her colony. Do not remove the stopper adjacent to the queen chamber, since this will release the queen immediately.  If the bees have not been given enough time to accept her, they will kill the new queen by what's called "bee balling."  This is a bee behavior where the worker bees surround the queen in a ball of fighting bees, killing and stinging the queen to death.

The queen is shipped with attendant bees in her little cage.  One problem that can sometimes hinder the release of the queen is dead attendant bees which block the queen from exiting her cage. This can be prevented by making sure the

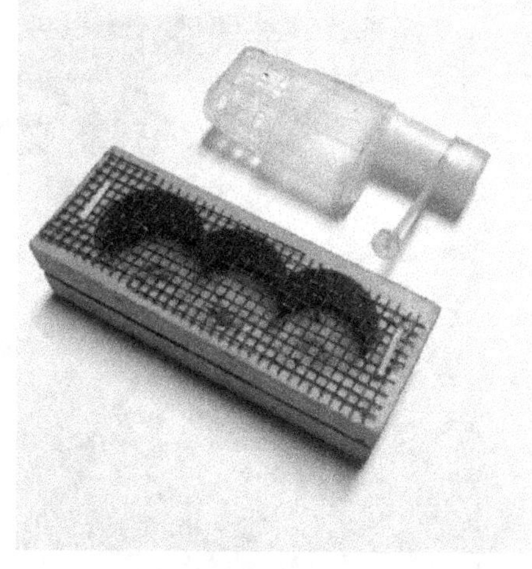

**Figure 32: Queen Cage Types**

candy filled exit tube or drilled hole is tilted slightly upward, so that any dead attendant bees will fall away from blocking her exit (See Figure 63).

Once the queen has been secured in her new home, the caged bee swarm can then be released in front of the colony.  The pheromone scent of the queen located inside the hive will draw the colony into their new home.  In this new home they will begin drawing out comb and chewing away the candy fondant blocking the queen's path.  This gradually releases the queen so that she can begin her egg laying and brood production.

Once the colony is in its new home, it's important to make certain that the entrance reducer is placed at its smallest opening size.  This is to prevent any nearby stronger colonies from robbing the new honey stores as the colony builds strength and gets established.

Another essential routine for the beekeeper is keeping the new colony fed with a 50:50 solution of sugar water.  This can be done using a frame feeder, Boardman feeder, or top feeder. (See Section 4f in Chapter 1 for feeder examples.)  When feeding, the beekeeper needs to make sure that syrup is not dripped around the colony.  Being sloppy with sugar syrup could attract a potentially stronger colony nearby and induce a "robbing" frenzy.

Once the new colony of package bees has built up sufficient drawn out comb for honey stores and brood production, the feeding can be discontinued and the bees will begin relying on local forage.  In some parts of the country like Texas, late summer can be a time of severe drought during which there is little to no nectar flow or pollen for the bees to gather. If for any reason you have a drought or dearth of nectar, it's important to feed the bees so that they can build up their winter stores.  Failing to ensure that your colony has at least 30-40 lbs of honey stores for the winter can potentially lead to the loss of your colony by starvation.

## 2. Ordering a Nuclear Colony.

One of the most effective and reliable ways of starting a new colony that I have found is by ordering a nuclear colony.  A nuclear colony usually consists of five frames of bees, brood and honey in a disposable box.  This includes a laying queen, two frames of brood, one frame of honey, one frame of pollen and an empty frame for expansion.  Although a nuclear colony is about 60% more costly than package bees, it is a more reliable means of starting your first colony.

**Figure 33: Four Nuclear Colonies on Stand**

The first step in ordering a nuclear colony is to check around your area for a bee supplier that has a good reputation for the quality and temperament of their bees. Some of the larger bee suppliers often produce a colony that has a hot temperament or may be a poor producer for the local area. For this reason it's important to check with other local beekeepers for their favorite source of bees.

Most areas usually have a local beekeeper's association that meets monthly. This is a great starting place for the beginner to find out where the bee suppliers are and when the nucs (nuclear colonies) come available. The more you develop a network of fellow beekeepers, the more successful you will be in meeting the particular challenges that are found in your area. For example, the North Dallas/Fort Worth area has very hot summers prone to drought, and very icy winters. This combination can be a great challenge for a colony's production of honey that is based on nectar flow, which is itself dependent on climate and rainfall.

Once you've ordered your nuclear colony, be sure to prepare your receiving 10 frame or 8 frame beehive for the 4 or 5 frame nuclear colony at least two weeks in advance.  This preparation needs to be accomplished well in advance of picking up the nuclear colony.  It will sometimes take new equipment a week or two to arrive, and it will take time to assemble and paint as well.  So, you want to make certain you're prepared with a home for your bees before they arrive.

On the day of arrival, during the daylight hours, transfer your nuclear colony frames to the new brood chamber.  If you have a 5 frame nuclear colony, and a 10 frame brood chamber, you'll need to provide an additional 5 empty frames that are carefully placed inside the hive, but on the outside of the other 4 or 5 new filled frames.  It's important to keep the bee cluster of this new colony together, not separated by empty frames.  Also, be sure to place the frames in the same order they were in the original nuc.  This is due to the sometimes slightly different contours of the frames.  Also be sure to not crush the queen as you put the frames next to each other.

The other key step is to provide either a top hive feeder, or frame feeder inside the brood chamber.  The 50:50 sugar syrup needs to be fed continuously for the next several weeks as the colony builds up.  You should check the colony at least once a week to make sure the colony is getting enough syrup, or nectar flow.  If the bees do not take the syrup after a week, chances are that your bees are getting a good flow of nectar that they prefer over the sugar syrup.  Once they stop taking the syrup, feeding can be stopped.

After the new colony has built out 80% of the brood chamber, it's time to provide a super so that the girls can continue their expansion of brood build up, and honey stores build up.

Failure to watch for build up that leads to overcrowding can result in the loss of your colony by swarming.  Always keep ahead of the bees by monitoring the health status of your colony.  One way to quickly check colony health is to lift up the backside of the colony in order to assess the weight that is being built up in your hive. When you lift the back of the hive, you are feeling approximately half the weight of the colony.

## 3.  Purchasing a full hive.

Another even easier way to acquire bees is to purchase a full 10 frame hive from either a bee vendor, or someone who may be interesting in selling their hives.  If you do the latter, be sure to inspect the bees with the seller to make certain that you're not getting someone else's problem colony.  The best way is to purchase from a certified bee vendor.  This is regulated by the State and provides the confidence that regular certified inspections bring.

## 4.  Collecting a Swarm.

If you happen to find out about a swarm which somehow comes available, this is one of the cheapest means of acquiring bees.  Still, if you choose this method, please be sure to have a more experienced beekeeper help you.  States usually require that beekeepers have a license for swarm pick-ups.

If you decide to use this method as your source of bees, once again you'll need to make certain to prepare the new colony's home well in advance of finding or acquiring the swarm.

Swarms are usually at their most docile states when they swarm.  This is because they've swarmed from the parent colony, leaving with bellies full of honey.  They do this in order to sustain the colony while searching for and establishing the colony at their new location.  However, beware of what is referred to as a "dry swarm."  This is when the colony for some reason has become depleted of their honey supply.  At this point the bees become very defensive, and can become dangerous if improperly handled or provoked. This is another reason for having a more experienced beekeeper along to help.  Make certain to wear all your equipment when handling a new unknown colony or swarm.

**Figure 34: Swarm Gathered on Tree**

One final word for acquiring a colony by swarm, I have seen cases where the initially docile swarm later becomes more aggressive once it's established and grown in size at its new home.  This can be due to the presence of Africanized drones in the area inseminating the queen, or it's possible that the swarm was originally feral and Africanized.  If you encounter this, it's important to re-queen the colony as soon as possible.

## 5. Trapping Out a Colony.

Another way of acquiring a colony is to trap out a population of bees from an existing colony that has located itself in a tree, house, or other permanent structure.  I actually used this method to start my first two colonies back in the late 1970's.

This method involves placing a funnel shaped screen cone over the entrance of the colony (See Figure 35). The bees are allowed to escape out of the colony through the screen wire cone, but are subsequently unable to re-enter the colony when they return.  This ends up producing a sizeable swarm on the outside of the cone.

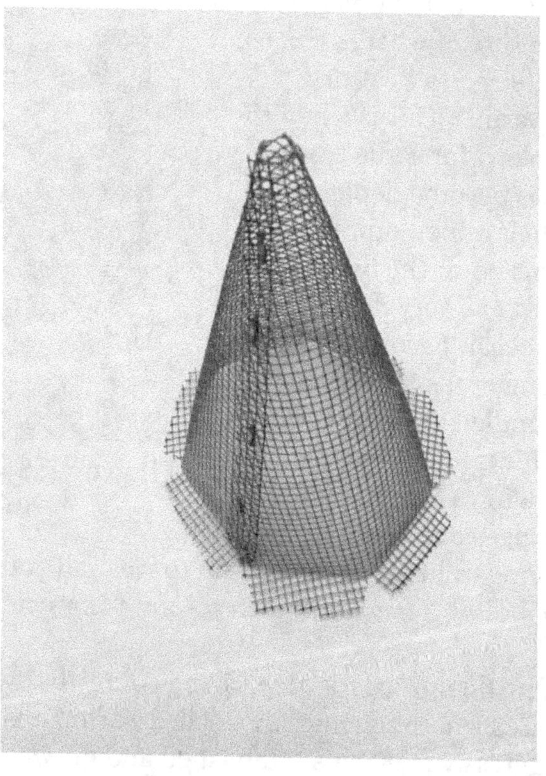

**Figure 35: Trap-out Cone**

They exit through the cone tip, but can't find their way back through the small hole.

A 5 frame nuc box is then placed close to the swarm hanging from the exit, and the evicted bees quickly adopt the nuc box as their new home.  Since the queen will not be likely to exit with the swarm, this method also requires that the beekeeper order or acquire a caged queen to provide to the newly established nuclear colony.  The down side of this method is that the former queen normally dies along with the remaining decimated colony due to attrition.  If the colony is being removed from a house, once the newly colony is moved to its new home, the old location should be opened and cleaned out of the old comb and dead bees.

# Chapter 4

## Basics for Setting up a Hive

One of the beauties of beekeeping is that you provide a structured environment for the bees to live and thrive, and they do the hard, laborious, and tedious work of pollen and nectar gathering.  This is not to minimize the hard work it will take for you to be a vigilant caretaker, along with the hard work of harvesting and extracting the surplus honey.  Rather, it is to emphasize and appreciate all the work that the bees are accomplishing that is humanly impossible to accomplish at such a microscopic and mind numbing numerical scale.  So, another one of the more important things you will have to do is set up a hive where the bees can thrive.

### 1. Location.

**a.  Where Do I Set up My Apiary?**  Just as the old real estate joke goes, there are three things which are essential for a good harvest: location, location, and location.  Where you locate your apiary can make a big difference in how big or how small your honey harvest is. The apiary or bee yard is the place where the

**Figure 36: Prairie Location of Colonies (Along Historic Chisholm Trail)**

beehives or colonies are kept.  In some areas, where local ordinances allow, this could be your backyard, while in others it might be near agricultural crops or orchards.

If you're keeping bees in your back yard, it's always important to check the local ordinances and restrictions.  In some communities, it is illegal to keep bees in your yard.  Some communities have laws restricting how close your colonies can be placed to a neighbor.  In any case, the county agricultural agent, or your local beekeeper's club or association are great sources for rules, laws and guidelines. It's important that you do your research with the local government, whether it's the county, city, township, or even homeowner's association. All of these entities usually have some restrictions on bees.  A good place to start looking is on the internet.

Once you've done your research on the local laws of the land, it's important to do a little local crop research.  Having local forage for the bees is essential for both the quantity and taste of your honey harvest.  Bees generally travel no more than 2-3 miles in a radius around your hive location.  So, it's wise to locate near fruit orchards, gardens where flowers are in abundance, or agricultural crops that are useful for honey production.  Table 1 shows a list of useful crops that can be targets for hive locations.

## Table 1 - Flowering Nectar & Pollen Sources

| Trees | Fruit Orchards | Agricultural Crops | Shrubs & Decorative | Wild Forage |
|---|---|---|---|---|
| Pecan | Pear | Cotton | Azalea | Dandelion |
| Maple | Orange | Sourgum | Sago Palm | Chickweed |
| Tupelo | Lemon | Soy | Lavender | Goldenrod |
| Crab Apple | Grapefruit | Buckwheat | Mountain Laurel | Milkweed |
| Sumac | Cherry | Red Clover | Crape Myrtle | Prickly Pear Cactus |
| Willow | Apple | Alfalfa | Honeysuckle | Palmetto |
| Catalpa | Plum | Peppermint | Lantana | Thistle |
| Hawthorne | Peach | Thyme | Sage | Guajillo |
| Holly | Blueberry | Sage | Salvia | Black Eyed Susan |
| Elm | Blackberry | Oregano | Chaste Tree - Vitex | Sunflower |
| Redbud | Strawberry | Rosemary | Hibiscus | Vetch |
| Mesquite | Rasberry | Garlic/Onion | Hyacinth | Larkspur |

**b. How do I Locally Situate my Colony?** Once you've selected the general locale of your apiary, you'll need to decide which way to face it, and where on the property you will place your colony or colonies. One of the more basic rules of thumbs for placing your colony is to have your entrance facing either East or South. This protects the entrance from facing the hot afternoon sun and the cold winter winds from the North.

Another consideration is how much area you have between you and your neighbors. It's particularly important not to face an entrance towards a nearby path, walkway or road. You can think of the entrance area of the colony as an airport runway. At key times during the day bees will be dropping out of the sky by the hundreds especially during a strong nectar flow. Consequently, you should locate the front of a hive no closer than 15 or 20 feet from a path or walkway. It's important to avoid walking directly in front of a colony for this same reason. Always approach a colony from behind.

If you don't have a 1 acre plus yard and are situated in tighter more restrained quarters, beekeepers will sometimes place a lattice or hedge a few feet away from the front of the hive. This creates an obstacle which will cause the bees to fly out of the hive in a more upward direction. Once they get up to a higher altitude, they will line up for their foraging runs.

**c. What About Placement on the Ground?** In many areas there are pests such as fire ants which can overwhelm and rob honey stores from the colony. This can end up weakening and killing the colony. For this reason I use a hive stand with ant moats. This method consists of a 2 x 4 construction of a rectangular frame support with anywhere from four to six legs. The legs are then placed in plastic coffee containers, which are filled with water. When kept full of water, the containers will keep out the ants. An example stand is shown in Figure 37. The hive stand should be constructed in such a way that the 150-250 lb hive is supported in a stable manner, and the top-heavy colony does not become a tipping hazard.

**Figure 37: Hive Stand with Ant Traps**

A set of plans for a stand can be found in Appendix A.

Some people have used concrete blocks, 4x4 pressure treated lumber, or even stands built with galvanized steel or pipes. Whatever the material, the main goal in placement is for the hive to be elevated from the ground.  This is to prevent moisture build up, to provide a barrier from ants and ground insects, and to provide a stable platform for the colony as it becomes heavy with brood and honey stores.  Notice in the photo above that the stand is placed behind a livestock fence. This is to prevent tipping or gnawing of woodenware by livestock

**2.  Langstroth Hive Set up.**  As discussed in Chapter 2 of this manual, there are four main parts to a Langstroth Hive Setup: The bottom board, the brood chamber, the super, the inner cover, and the top cover.  One of the decisions you'll need to make when getting started is whether to go with **8 frame** equipment or 10 frame equipment.

The traditional Langstroth hives usually employ 10 frames in each brood chamber or super.  However, this makes hive segments heavy to pick up and manipulate.  If you have back problems like me, the 8 frame equipment is probably your best choice.  The 10 frame supers are 25% heavier than the 8 frame supers.  This can make a big difference.  A medium frame usually weighs about 3 lbs. Consequently, lifting a medium super with 8 frames involves 24 lbs plus the weight of the equipment, while the 10 frame

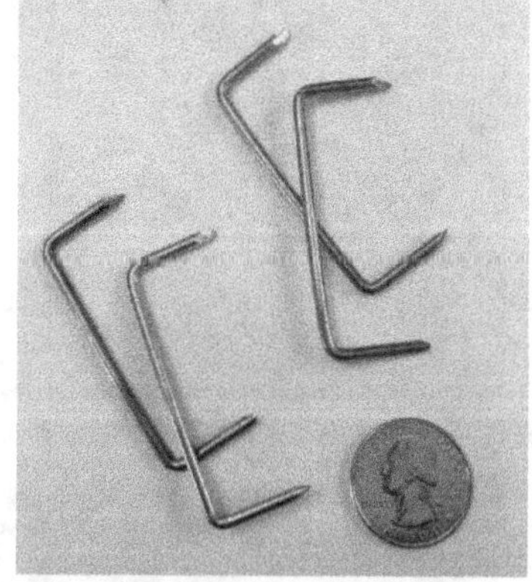

**Figure 38: Hive Staples**

super is 30 lbs plus the weight of the equipment.

When you initially set up your colony, you'll want to only set up the brood chamber and have the super prepared and ready for later.  The brood box is set or nailed to the bottom board using **hive staples**.  If you're starting your colony with a 4 or 5-frame nuclear colony, you'll want to add however many additional frames are needed to fill the 8 or 10 frame equipment.  On one hand, it's important to keep your colony in an enclosure of a size that will not lead to having so

**Figure 39: Bottom Board Attached with Hive Staples**

much room inside that they can't defend it against hive beetles or wax moths.  On the other hand, you want to make certain that you don't crowd the bees so much that swarming becomes a problem.

The Goldilocks' rule for room in the hive is, once your colony has filled out 80% of the frames in a brood chamber or super, it's time to provide more room for expansion.  So, on a ten frame colony, once your brood chamber has grown from 5 drawn-out frames to 8 drawn-out frames, it's time to add a super.  For a strong and healthy colony that's experiencing a good nectar flow, a full super can be drawn out and filled in a just a couple of weeks.  Consequently, during spring and other known nectar flows, it will be important to regularly check your colony every two weeks.

Another thing you'll want to include in your initial set-up is either a frame feeder, or a top feeder. It's important to provide a solution of 50:50 sugar to water syrup as a feed. This will stimulate brood production and the drawing out of comb. If the bees are experiencing a nectar flow, the bees may ignore your syrup for a while. However, it's important to check the syrup levels at least on a weekly basis for your new colony. You'll also need to provide the syrup during dry or dearth periods for your area.

**3. Set up for Nuclear Colony on Arrival Day.** On the day that you receive your 4 or 5 frame nuclear colony, you'll need to set your closed nuc on the ground next to their new 8 or 10 frame home. Remove the top and inner cover of Langstroth hive, and ensure that the proper number of frames are there in the hive box. If you're using a frame feeder, you'll need to reduce the number of frames by 1 frame, depending upon the width of your frame feeder. Boardman feeders can also be used, but this is not recommended due to the risk of initiating a robbing frenzy from another stronger colony nearby.

It's advisable to have your 50:50 sugar syrup pre-prepared and ready to pour into your feeder. When using a frame feeder, I prefer having the frame feeder with syrup in the hive body before I begin placing the frames of brood in the

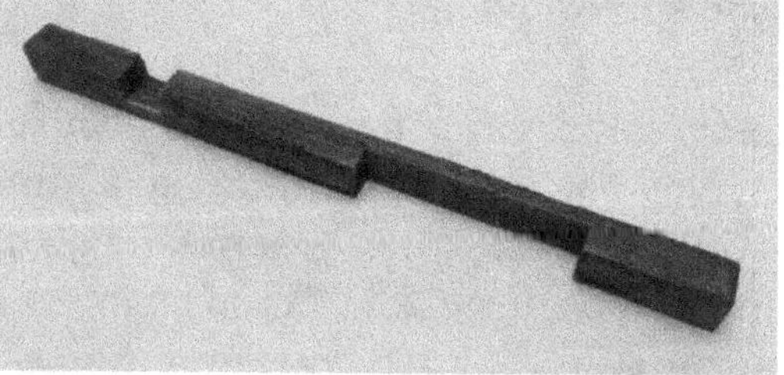

**Figure 40: Entrance Reducer (8 Frame)**

hive. I usually place the frame feeder on the far side of the brood chamber away from the reduced entrance of the colony. I also always use the smallest entrance setting for the entrance reducer. This helps prevent robbing by other stronger colonies and helps the guard bees to have a smaller entrance to defend.

A top feeder is located the furthest from the entrance, but needs to be filled as the final step before closing up the colony.  If there are entrance vents in your top cover, you may want to temporarily block them off so that other bees won't raid the top feeder through the openings.

When you begin placing your frames in the new hive body, be certain to keep the same order of frames that you had in the nuclear colony.  This is because the bees sometimes draw out a slightly contoured surface that matches up with the adjacent frame.  Re-arranging frames can sometimes create closer gaps between frames, which can end up squishing bees, or even the queen.

Whenever removing the first frame of a hive box, it is good practice to remove either the end frame or 2$^{nd}$ frame first. This is because the queen is usually not located in this position.  If you attempt to remove a frame in the middle of the box, before being able to move the frame over, you may end up "rolling the queen." Since the queen is larger than the other bees, she can end up getting squished and killed by the careless beekeeper.  Caution, and close observation of the frames as you remove them can prevent this potentially colony-destroying event.

Start your colony with two empty frames on the side closest to the reduced entrance. Then, from the end of the nuc, carefully pull the first frame from the nuc box, and place it next to the two empty frames.  Continue, by carefully sliding each subsequent frame sideways away from its neighboring frame, and then up and out of the nuc.  In a similar but opposite fashion, place the frame initially away from its adjacent frame in the new colony, and carefully slide the frame into position. When you do this, be careful to preserve the "bee space" between each frame. If you have kept the same order, you can usually see evidence of wax features that fit together like a honeycomb puzzle.

Once you have all 5 frames in, plus the 2 initial empty frames, you'll be about 2 frames away from your frame feeder. If you can fit both frames without squeezing the other frames too much, go ahead and put both in. However, if it seems too crowded, hold off a few weeks on putting the 9th frame in until you remove the frame feeder. At that time, put in the 9th and 10th frames. If you do this, be sure to slide the frame feeder a little closer to the last frame so that you have a single bee space. This will prevent the bees from filling another slat of honeycomb in the larger space.

Once all of your frames, feeder, and entrance reducer are in place, you can place the inner cover and telescoping cover on your colony. Then, it's time to give the bees a few days to get settled in their new home. Give the bees at least 5-7 days before disturbing them. At the same time, make certain that you've given them at least a gallon of syrup feed so that they can begin building comb.

# Chapter 5

## Maintaining a Healthy Colony

Back in 1974 when I was getting started in beekeeping, it was very simple to keep a colony of bees healthy and alive. However, in today's environment with the threat of hive beetles, Varroa mites, Israeli bee virus, Africanized bees, colony collapse disorder and a host of newly invented pesticides, it can be extremely difficult just to keep your bees alive. However, here are a few things you can do to help your "girls" thrive, so that they'll all be humming "Stayin' Alive."

**1. Feed Regularly.** If you did nothing other than this one thing, you would significantly enhance your colony's probability of survival. Feeding includes various solutions of sugar syrup, candy boards, and pollen patties. In general, there are key times and seasons when it is especially helpful to feed your bees.

**a. New Colony.** Whenever you have a new colony or starter nuc, you'll need to make sure that your bees are provided with a 50:50 sugar to water syrup solution. Pollen patties are another good supplemental food that you can give to a new colony.

Pollen patties are usually made from a mixture of soy flour, brewer's yeast, and sugar syrup, which is rolled into a flat dough-like form. Some will add medicinal additives such as Honey Bee Healthy, to help stave off viruses and other bee ailments. The ingredients shown in Appendix B are mixed together in a bowl like cookie dough. An 8 to 16 oz patty of the dough is placed between two sheets of wax paper, and then rolled out to a thickness of about 3/16 of an inch, being about 4 inches in width, and 8 inches in length.  This is so that it can fit between the bee space over your brood chamber.

After the pollen patties are prepared, trimming away the excess wax paper sandwich, the patties are then taken to the colonies.  Patties are then placed somewhere near the cluster, usually over the tops of the frames in the bee space.

In addition to the syrup, the pollen patties help stimulate brood production, by helping to simulate the spring-like conditions of the pollen and nectar flow.  This is especially important as the bees get situated in their new location. It's also essential if there is not a good pollen and nectar flow when your new colony arrives.

**b. Summer Droughts or Dearths.**  Whenever there is drought, or dearth of nectar flow, it is essential to feed syrup.  If your colony has grown light on honey stores, failure to provide the needed syrup for honey production can be fatal to your colony.

**c.  Winter Hybernations.** As your colony goes into the winter cluster, feeding nectar becomes problematic.  One of the biggest problems bees have during winter in trying to cope with the cold weather is moisture.  If the moisture levels get too high in a colony during the cold weather, this condition alone can wipe out a colony

The **winter cluster** is a tight swarm like formation of bees where the colony forms a ball shape mass amidst the frames of the colony.  The cluster is somewhat of a heating core that protects the queen at its nucleus.  Whenever the outside temperature drops below 55°F, the bees will form this cluster to preserve the energy of the colony.  Bees on the outside of the cluster will rotate toward the inside of the cluster on a regular basis as the bees form a tight linked cluster like a swarm.

The queen is kept at the center of the cluster at a warm temperature of approximately 94°F. Bees in the cluster generate heat by friction through movement of the wings and legs. While in the winter cluster, the colony consumes less honey than during warmer temperatures. Although the bees are technically not "hibernating", the winter cluster is a similar concept for energy conservation.

When bees bring in nectar during the summer, they must dehydrate the nectar down to its proper viscosity or water content so that it becomes the syrupy form of honey. During this time, you will see worker bees at the entrance fanning the front of the hive. This is done to create good circulation of air which provides for efficient evaporation of water across the surface of the nectar-filled honeycomb. When bees are in their winter cluster, fanning to create wind currents would bring cold air into the colony, which could lead to the colony freezing. For this reason colonies cannot efficiently dry honey when temperatures are below 40°F. Even more important, bees usually will not break cluster until the outside temperature is above 50°F.

Consequently, beekeepers have found that providing "candy boards" at the top of the colony, under the cover, provide a more dried form of needed sugars for the bees to feed on. In fact, since dry sugar or candy is hygroscopic, the candy helps to reduce the humidity in the hive as an added benefit. See Appendix C for recipe and plans.

During the latter part of winter, beekeepers will often provide pollen patties for the colonies. This will give your colony a head start on the brood build up, before the pollen and nectar flow begins in the spring.

**d.  Fall Build Up**.  Another important time for regular feeding is during fall build up.  As the temperatures begin to drop and nectar sources become less plentiful, it's important for your colony to go into its cluster period with a strong population and sufficient honey stores.  One quick way to check the status of your colony is to carefully lift the back side of your colony up to see how much stored honey the colony has.  If you can't lift the back up the colony probably has at least 40-50 lbs of honey.  However, if you can easily lift the back bottom board and colony up, you probably have deficient honey stores.

If the colony appears light, you need to perform a hive inspection to see what's going on inside the hive.  Is the colony queenless?  Is there a low production of brood, possibly due to a failing queen?  If you determine the colony is on its way out, it may be advisable to find the failing queen, kill her, and merge the remaining bees and honey stores with another week colony.  However, make sure you have a new queen before you take this final step. (For more information on merging colonies, see Chapter 7 on Winterizing Your Colony.)

Another possible solution for strengthening your weak colony is to begin feeding both 2:1 sugar water syrup, and administering a one pound pollen patty.  The syrup will help the colony build up honey stores, and the pollen patties will help stimulate brood production.

**e.  Post-Extraction**.  The other helpful time to routinely feed your colony is after you have harvested honey.  Although the bees may be able to fill the drawn comb fairly easily from the local nectar flow, you might live in an area where there is a dearth or shortage of nectar flow after the early spring nectar flow. If this is the case, it is especially important to provide sugar syrup as feed. However, unlike the 2:1 sugar to water ratio used in the fall and cooler months, a 50:50 sugar to water ratio should be used during the warmer months.

**2. Check for Varroa Mites**. Over the last several years, an emerging problem for American beekeepers has been the arrival of Varroa mites. Female Varroa mites are about the size of a head of a pin, being approximately 1/16 of an inch in diameter, while the males are about half that size at about 1/32 of an inch in diameter. Varroa mites can often be found attaching themselves to the back of the thorax of the host bee. Varroa mites will literally

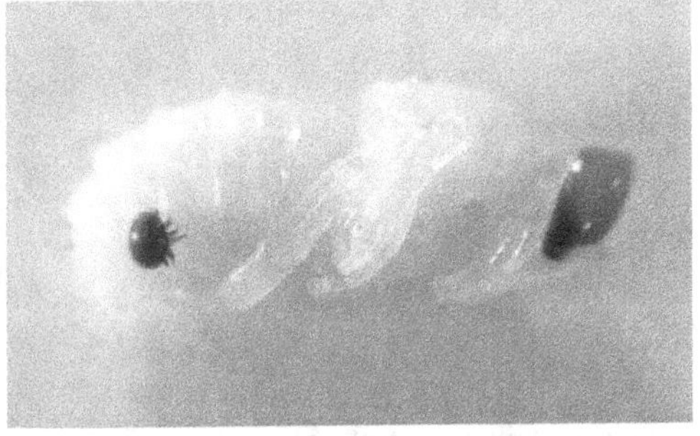

**Figure 41: Varroa Mite on Drone Brood Abdomen**

suck the life out of bees, and can even wipe out a colony if it becomes infested.

Another sign of Varroa mites will be the appearance of infant workers or drones with tiny deformed wings at the entrance of the colony. These deformed bees can also sometimes be found on the brood frames as well. The deformity is the result of the presence of a bee virus that is itself carried by the host Varroa mite.

If a colony is becoming infected with Varroa mites, the mites can also be found attached to drone larvae inside their capped cells. Carefully removing and inspecting drone larvae from their capped cells is another way of checking for Varroa mites. The mites look like tiny reddish brown or light tan seeds upon the body of the drone larva.

If your hive has a Varroa screen on the bottom board, and is equipped with a checker board mite count board, you can check for the presence of mites on the board itself. Another more intrusive method is to take a cluster of about 20 bees and shake them in a jar with powdered sugar. The bees and powdered sugar are then shaken out on a white sheet of paper. The powdered sugar helps to dislodge the mites from the bees, and allows you to count them after they have fallen off on the white sheet of paper. In all these different methods, it is important to take steps to treat for mites if you find your colony is infested with Varroa mites. Treatment methods can be found in Chapter 9 of this book.

**Figure 42: Sugar Shake Jar**

**3. Provide Small Hive Beetle Traps.** Another one of the several scourges that has descended upon the North American bee population is the Small Hive Beetle (SHB). The SHB was originally discovered in Sub-Saharan Africa and named *Aethina tumida* by entomologist Andrew Murry in 1867. The SHB looks somewhat like a completely black version of a lady bug. However, these are not at all like the cute and beneficial lady bug who

**Figure 43: Workers Herding Hive Beetle**

graces the garden with her helpful elimination of aphids and her other organic  pest-controlling qualities. Rather, the SHB is a scurrying pest that can invade and infect a colony to the point of its slimy destruction.

If you have a SHB presence, they are usually first noticed as scurrying 3/16" diameter black dots about  the size of a chad made from a hole punch on your inner cover. When you discover them, it is advisable to use your hive tool to immediately squish these troublesome intruders. Over the last several years, beekeepers have discovered that bees manage and fight off hive beetles by cornering and propalyzing the intruders into what have been dubbed as "beetle jails" or propalis compartments. Unfortunately, when you open up the inner cover and pry apart frames, this can often releases the beetles in a sufficient number that can at times lead to SHB eggs being laid in and around the honeycomb stores.

Once the prolific female SHB lays her undetected eggs in the honeycomb and hive surfaces, SHB larvae will eat their way through the colonies wax honeycomb stores. As they eat their way through, the beetles defecate and spoil the honey stores into a slimy fermented mess. If a population of SHB larvae infects a hive, it can lead to the collapse and complete ruin of the infected colony. The SHB larvae usually appear like small thin maggots, similar to but smaller than wax moth larvae.

There are a couple of things which I have found to be helpful in combating the presence of SHB. First, small hive beetles do not seem to like hives that are placed in a sunny location. They appear to prefer colonies located in shady areas. Shade seems to be beneficial to the lifecycle of their larvae, which after sliming a colony will drop down into the ground where they pupate and metamorphose into their adult form. So, when choosing a location in hot places like Texas, find a location near a tree which will provide afternoon sun shade, while allowing a good solar exposure during the earlier morning and noon hours. This provides an excellent environment that seems to stave off the SHB.

Second, if you have no choice but to locate in an

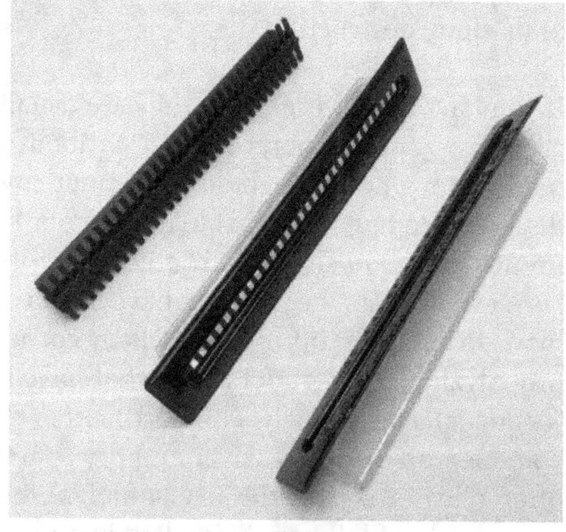

**Figure 44: Beetle Traps**

area where you end up with a significant population of SHB, I've found that SHB traps are an excellent help to the bees in the elimination of the pests. There are a number of trap designs which can be placed in the space between frames. One trap design has small slots along the top surface, beneath which lies a small reservoir for vegetable oil. This oil becomes a proverbial LaBrea Tar Pit for the SHB. There's nothing better than to lift the see-through Beetle Trap and see dozens of beetles submerged and drowned in their oil bath. It is important to clean out and replenish beetle traps with new oil every few weeks. Otherwise, the traps become so congested that the drowned beetles fill up the trap and beetles can simply crawl back out without being submerged in the oil.

One thing that seems to be especially helpful in luring beetles into the traps is to add a few thin slivers of apple, or a few drops of vinegar into the oil. This appears to be an attractant for the beetles which makes the traps more efficient and is well worth the extra effort.

There are a host of different types of beetle traps. In addition to the variety described above, there are some that are placed under the bottom board, having a larger reservoir. In either case it is advisable to have a few traps on hand either to act as a prevention or cure, should your colony be faced with a growing SHB population.

**4. Provide Ant Traps.** In the great state of Texas, we have the unfortunate distinction of being the fire ant capital of the US. If a nearby fire ant colony discovers your bee colony as a source of food, it can quickly lead to the depletion of your colony's honey stores. When that happens, the colony will usually swarm to another location, leaving behind the very un-neighborly ants. Consequently, one of the ways you can help protect your bees against an invading army of hungry ants is by providing ant traps. There are a number of hive stands that are on the market which have built in ant traps using either vegetable oil or water.  However, I've found one economic solution is to build a stand out of 2 x 4's with legs that can be immersed in large plastic coffee cans filled with water (See Figure 45).  As long as the cans are kept filled, these coffee cans provide an effective moat which will cut off the ant's access to your hive and honey stores.

An important thing to watch for when using the ant traps is the accumulation of leaves or debris.  If debris builds up, this can render your ant moat useless, and provide a new pathway for the ants onto your hive stand and into your hive.  For this reason, regular observation and maintenance of ant traps is essential. Plans with dimensions are included in Appendix A.

Figure 45: Homemade Hive Stand with Ant Traps

# Chapter 6

## Harvesting Honey Stores

**1. Preparing to Harvest Honey**.  The first year you start your colony, you'll likely want to harvest some of the honey.  However, even though you're seeing amazing stores of honey being put up by your bees, you would be wise to wait and to work on building a strong and well-established colony before removing honey surplus.

As the bees bring in nectar, they will be drawing out new comb on new frames, or storing nectar in previously depleted cells from winter.  One way of thinking about how a colony works is to consider the three primary functions or products of the colony.  Using honey, pollen and nectar stores, bees will be producing  brood, comb, or honey.  The ideal situation for honey production is to have a strong colony of bees, where there is existing comb.  This way most of the resources of the colony can be spent on honey production.

If there is a shortage of wax honeycomb, the bees will use part of the nectar and honey to produce wax.  The rule of thumb for wax production is that it takes approximately 7 lbs of honey for the bees to produce 1 lb of wax.   When you look at it from this perspective, you realize how valuable your honeycomb is, and how important it is to help the bees protect it from the wax moths.

**2. Deciding When to Harvest Honey**.  Once your colony is built up to at least one full brood chamber and one full medium-depth super of honey, you should feel free to harvest any of the excess stores of honey above this amount.  Although there are some beekeepers who have multiple harvests during the spring and early Fall, here in Texas I choose to harvest honey once per year in early to mid-July. By this time there has usually been a good spring build-up of both brood and honey, and the colony should be ready to give up some of its capped-over honey.

There are some beekeepers who will draw the honey stores down very low in a colony. However, when beekeepers do this in an area where there is a summer drought, or a dearth of nectar flow, a hive that is not being fed can end up collapsing and dying. This is because the queen will usually slow down her production of brood during drought periods to keep the population of bees from becoming too much higher than the available stores of honey. For this reason, experienced beekeepers frequently recommend that you feed a colony immediately after extracting honey.

Another important factor to consider when removing frames of honeycomb from your hive is the percentage of capped honeycomb. Oftentimes you will see areas of capped honey underneath or around areas of uncapped honey. In this case the bees are either using the uncapped comb as a food source for brood, or they are still in the process of drying out the moisture from the nectar in order to produce the final product, honey.

One rule of thumb that beekeepers have used is making certain that at least 85% of your frame has capped honey stores, with less than 15% of uncapped honey. The reason this is so important is that honey which has not been fully cured, has too high of a water content, and will likely ferment in the container. This is often evidenced by fermentation bubbles and a sour fermented smell to the honey. For this reason, I try to make certain that 95-100% of my frames are drawn out and capped. I tend to leave frames that have only been partially drawn out and capped as a food source and working honeycomb for the bees.  Once you've reached a satisfactory level of capped over honey, you're now ready to begin your honey harvest.

**2.  Removing Capped Honeycomb From Your Colony.**  On the day that you're ready to remove capped honey frames from your colony, or colonies, you'll need to make certain that you are ready to implement steps 3 -7 within an approximate 48 hour period.  This is because leaving any of your frames for a prolonged period with or without honey can lead to a hatching out of wax moth larvae, and the rapid destruction of your valuable honey and/or wax.

As long as your honeycomb is stored on an active colony, the bees are constantly inspecting and cleaning the surface of the comb for invading pests.  Whether it's a SHB small hive beetle, SHB larva, or wax moth larva, the bees are working to protect the honey stores.  Once the bees are removed from the frames, you are now in danger of honey and wax devouring pests destroying your harvest.  For this reason you should work quickly and efficiently, and have a plan for all 7 steps.

There are several different ways you can remove the bees from the frames.  One method is to remove frames one by one to an empty super, brushing off the bees as you go.  This method ensures that you are only removing frames that are ready for harvest.  It's a good idea to have a solid catch base below the harvested frames, so that other bees do not enter from below and begin robbing honey from your harvested frames.  A cover over the top, or sheet of canvas is also helpful to protect the newly harvested frames from attracting nearby bees.

If you're dealing with more than 5 colonies, you may want to use a more efficient technique.  Many beekeepers use a bee repellant, such as Fisher's Bee Quick sprayed on a vapor board.  This is solution of natural oils and extracts that acts as a repellant to the bees.  I use a fume board on top of the super

**Figure 46: Homemade Fume Board**

I want to remove, and a bee trap board beneath the super I want to remove.  The fume board is usually similar to a migratory top but with a sheet of burlap or other absorbent fabric stapled to the underside of the lid.

The fume board is placed over the colonies, with the bee trap board underneath. Usually by about 10-15

**Figure 47: Bee Traps**

minutes after placement of the fume board, most of the bees have evacuated to the brood chamber and supers beneath the trap board. The trap board allows the bees to travel down and out, but not up and back. The bees travel down through the hole on the top side of the trap and exit through the maze. Because of the sharp turns at the end of the triangular shaped trap, the bees can't find their way back up. Traps can also be used with a plastic trap insert that fits in the inner cover. The inner cover with trap is placed below the super to be removed and the fume board above.

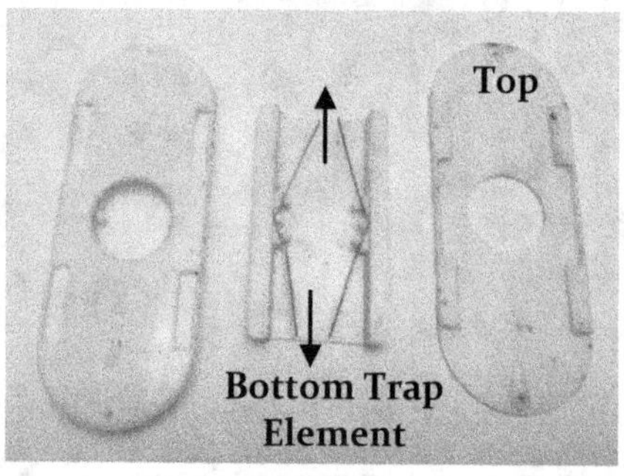


**Figure 48: Bee Trap Disassembled to show One Way Trap Feature**

If you don't use queen excluders, it is important to make certain that you haven't included brood frames in this method of removal.

### 3. Transporting & Short Term Storing of Honeycomb.

Once you have removed the frames from the colony and set them aside in a cleaned out super, you'll need to transport them back to the place of extraction. If you're only transporting one or two supers, you might be able to carry these by hand back to your truck or vehicle. However, since even a typical 8 frame medium super can weigh anywhere from 25-30 lbs, carrying 3 or 4 supers requires additional equipment.

In moving 2 or more supers of honey, I usually use a hand
dolly with a drip board set at the bottom of the dolly to catch
any honey that drips from the frames.  If you're moving
frames out in a field where car or truck access is not possible,
you'll probably need to use a dolly or a cart that has wheels
large enough so that they can negotiate the soft ground.  I've
found that carts with at least a 3 ½ in. wheel width and 10 in.
diameter are able to carry the load of 4 or 5 supers, and not
sink into the ground too much.

Once you get the honey stores to the location where you'll do
the extraction, you'll want to get the uncapping and
extraction done as soon as possible.  As mentioned in step 2,
leaving honey stores without the protection of the bees can
lead to the sacking of your honey stores by wax moth larvae,
ants, or other pests.

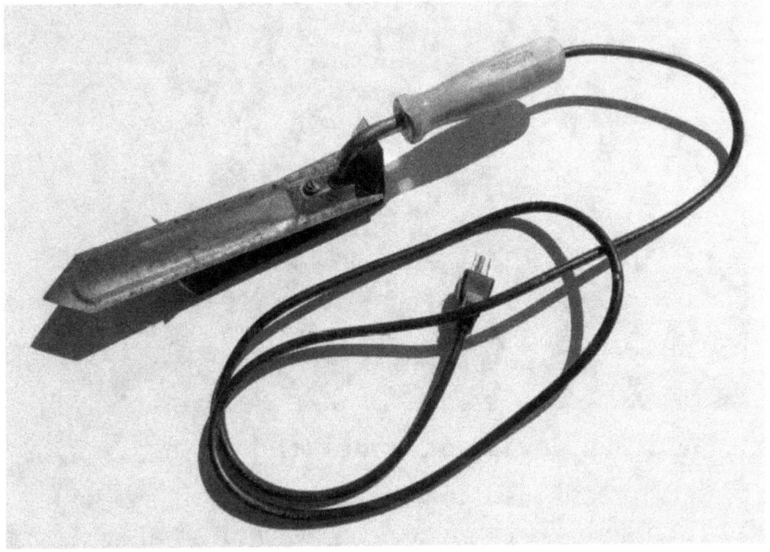

**Figure 49: Heated Uncapping Knife**

**4. Uncapping Honey.** There are a few ways of uncapping honey to prepare the frames for extraction in an extractor.

**Figure 50: Uncapping Honey (Hot Knife)**

The most commonly used tool in uncapping is the hot knife. This is a double-bladed knife which plugs into a wall outlet to provide a heated blade that can then easily slice through the very tops of the honeycomb caps.

Another simple method of capping is the use of a cold knife.
You can order either the hot or cold uncapping knives from
bee supply houses.  I've found that a sharp serrated bread
knife is very effective at uncapping honey.

Using whatever knife you choose, the frame is placed over an
uncapping tub or bin, which itself has an attached wooden
cross piece to set one of the sides of the frame upon, while
holding the other ear of the frame in a slightly angled upward
direction.

I usually start from the bottom of a frame and work the knife
in an upward direction so that the thin layer of honeycomb
caps fold out and into the uncapping bin.  I then rotate the
frame to the other side and do the same upward cutting
motion to remove the other side as well. (Some prefer a
downward cutting motion.)
It's always important to
double check and make
sure that you've uncapped
both sides of a frame.  If
you miss one side of a
frame, you'll find during
extraction that the capped
honey will produce an
imbalance in your extractor
as the other frames empty.

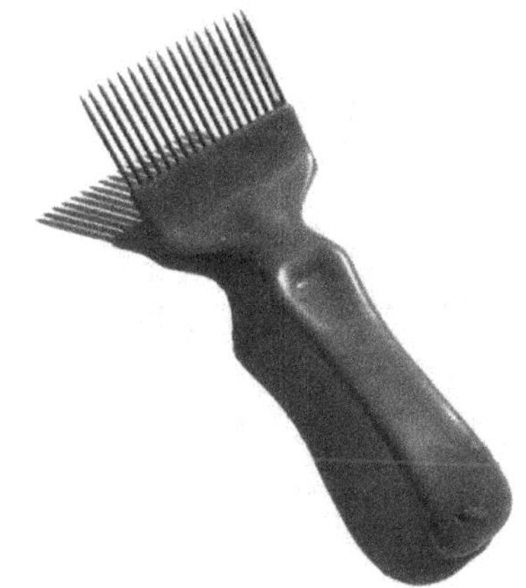

**Figure 51: Capping Scratcher**

Another thing I've
noticed that affects
uncapping is how shallow or how proud the honeycomb sits
in the frame.  This usually depends on how closely you have
spaced your frames.  Spacing frames too far apart can lead to
the bees building multiple layers of honeycomb between the
frames.  Spacing frames too close can lead to the honeycomb

surface setting too low between the frame rails.  When this occurs, the frame rails keep the knife from getting down into the top layer of the honeycomb cappings.

When honeycomb is too shallow in the frame, there are a couple of tools that are helpful in getting the frame uncapped. The first tool is an uncapping comb, or capping scratcher (See Figure 51). The comb can be used to either scratch the surface of the honeycomb to remove the cappings, or by angling the comb, to gently lift the cappings from the surface of the honeycomb.

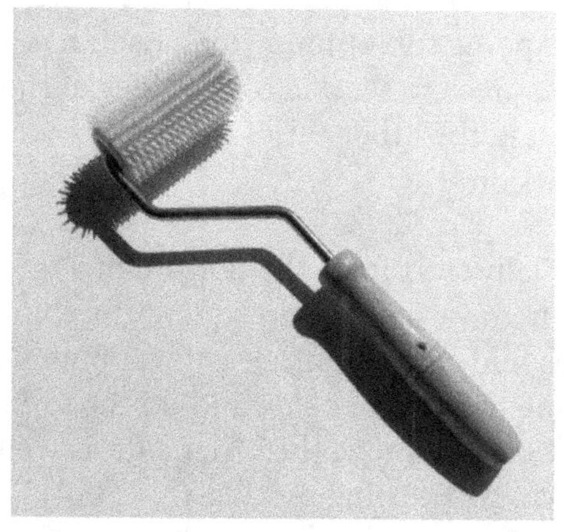

**Figure 52: Uncapping Tool**

The other relatively new uncapping tool is the uncapping roller (See Figure 52).  This has equally spaced brush- like tines that can be rolled over the surface of the honeycomb to prick the surface of each honeycomb cell.  Once the frames have been uncapped by one or more of the above techniques, the extraction can begin.

**5.  Extraction Methods.**  There are two basic means of extracting honey that have been used for several centuries in beekeeping: conventional rotational extraction, and pressure methods of extraction.

**a.  Conventional Rotational Extraction.**  The first method of extraction is probably the most efficient method of extraction. However, this method does involve equipment, which can be somewhat expensive. Rotational extraction involves the use of a containment drum, in which the frame, or frames are rotated either by a mechanical hand crank or an electric motor.

**Figure 53: Radial Extractor w/Frame Position**

Frames are placed inside the extractor drum in a basket or frame cage, which allows the frames to be spun to extract the honey from the cells by centrifugal force. There are two methods of rotational extraction: radial and tangential. In radial extraction the frames are oriented like spokes on a wheel and are spun around a central axis (see Figure 53). In tangential extraction the frames are oriented in a basket or cage inside the perimeter of the drum (see Figure 55). Tangential extraction involves an additional step of rotating the frames to the other side, once the external side of the frame is emptied.

To extract frames using a centrifugal extractor, the uncapped frames are placed in the extractor's basket or rack. For radial extractors, the frames need to be placed with the top of the frame facing toward the outside of the drum. Since honeycomb cells are slightly canted in an upward direction,

**Foundation Comb     Natural Comb**
**Figure 54: Honeycomb Cross Sections**
**(Arrow on Comb Shows Sling Direction)**

frames need to be placed in an outward direction so that the viscous honey will efficiently draw out due to the radial centrifugal force (See Figure 54). Placement in the opposite inward or "down" direction would tend to push the honey against the center of the frame, and could tend to tear up the honeycomb if extracted at a high rate of speed (RPM).

Tangential Extraction Tip:  Frames should be placed with the bottom of the frame acting as the leading edge of the spin.  This will allow for more efficient extraction of the honey, as shown in Figure 55.  Flip the frame in an up an out direction, rather than simply spinning by a flip inside the basket.  This is because in a tangential extractor one side faces inward, and holds the honey.  Simply rotating will put the frame in the opposite direction with the top of the frame as the leading edge.  The extra effort will be worth the more efficient extraction of viscous honey.

Smaller hand cranked extractors are typically tangential.  This is because the smaller two or three framed extractors can be placed inside a smaller diameter drum, while the radial extractors usually require the radius of the drum to be at least depth of the frame.  For this reason, many smaller radial

**Figure 55: Tangential Hand Crank Extractor**

frame extractors are for shallow or medium frame supers only, while deep frames require a change out to a tangential deep frame basket.

When extracting with a tangential extractor, it is especially

**Figure 56: Typical Extraction Set-up**

important not to accelerate the spinning of the extractor too aggressively. Since you are extracting one side of the frame at a time, you will have the weight of the opposite side of the frame pressing against the center of the frame wanting to push out. Depending on whether there is a screen basket or frame cage, comb breakage can be particularly problematic if you are using non-reinforced wax foundation and no basket for the comb to press against. Foundation is usually reinforced with either wire supports or a plastic underlying foundation, so you will want to make sure you use reinforced foundation if you plan to extract using a tangential extractor without a screen cage. Once you've done a few of either of the two methods, tangential, or radial, you will begin to develop a feel for how slowly or quickly to ramp up your extraction, followed by a high speed rotation once the frames are practically empty.  The final high speed step helps to extract the last drops of honey from the comb.

Extractors need to be securely mounted to a solid base so that the vibration of the spinning frames does not shake the extractor into an unstable state.  For this reason, extractors are usually equipped with some form of tie down chains or fittings, in order to provide stability to the unit.  The bottom of the extractor and honey gate are usually placed a sufficient distance from the ground to enable a 5 gallon pale with filtering screens to be placed directly underneath the honey gate.

As the honey is centrifugally spun from the frames, the harvest flows down to the bottom of the extractor, out the gate and into the filter pans.  Beekeepers will often use cheese cloth, or woman's stocking placed over the top to filter out any wax or bee particles from the honey.  Some beekeepers will use finer mesh screens to remove pollen.  This tends to provide better shelf life with regards to inhibiting crystallization.  However, many local honey beekeepers consider a small amount of pollen in the honey to be a valuable product to those who use honey for the benefits of its pollen content.

**b.  Pressure Methods of Extraction.**  Another method that has been used in primitive areas of beekeeping is honey extraction by pressure.  This usually involves a small mechanical press, like that used in the extraction of grape juice from grapes in winemaking.  This method is used in frameless, foundationless, or top bar hives, and is also used to extract honeycomb slats harvested from feral colonies.  In this method sections of honeycomb are wrapped in cheesecloth and placed in the extraction press. The worm gear is gradually dialed down until all of the honey is squeezed out of the press, and only wax remains.

**6. Returning Empty Drawn Frames to Your Colony**. Returning your empty drawn frames to your colony really should be done as soon as possible – hopefully, immediately after you have extracted your honey into the larger storage containers. The reason this is so important is that the empty honeycomb is a prime target for wax moth  or hive beetle larvae.

There are oftentimes microscopic moth or beetle eggs which have been laid by invading pests.  As long as the bees are managing the combs, any hatch-out is quickly eliminated by the colony's bee population.  However, when there are no bees on the comb, the larvae can quickly feed and grow as they damage the unwatched honeycomb.  For this reason returning your comb to a strong and active colony is an essential part of harvesting honey.

**7. Bottling Honey.** After the honey has been extracted from the comb and filtered into a large container; the next step will be bottling honey. One of the keys to efficient bottling of honey is really tied to

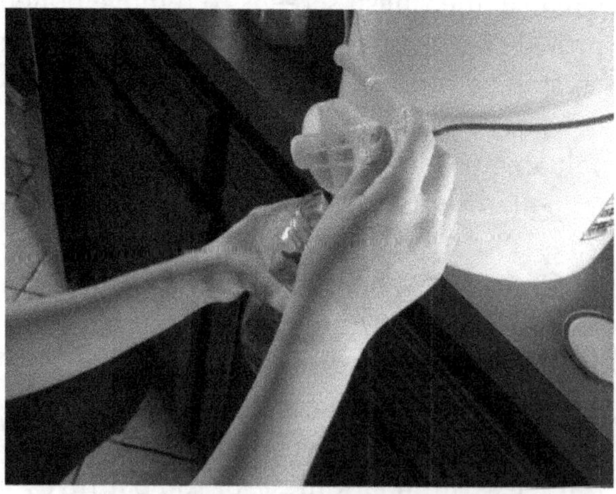

**Figure 57: Bottling Honey w/ Honey Gate & 5 Gal Container**

the larger storage container that your honey is extracted into. One of the most convenient methods of handling extracted honey is through the use of 5 gallon pails with a honey gate installed in the bottom of the pail.

Storage pails with honey gates can be purchased at a reasonable price from your bee supply house.  These sometimes include a three stage filter basket that is placed in the mouth of the container.  The filter baskets are ordered such that as the honey drips from the extraction gate, the honey enters the course sieve first, then the medium sieve which filters out slightly smaller particles than the course, and then finally through the smallest sieve at the bottom of the filter stack.  Filtering in this way keeps the finer filters from clogging.

There are a variety of plastic and glass bottles that can be purchased from bee supply houses for storage and marketing of honey.  However, 8 oz, 16 oz, and 32 oz Mason jars can be purchased at the local store at a fairly reasonable price, and these provide a great way to divide your harvest into reasonably sized storage jars for distribution and sales.  Once you have your honey harvest bottled, and left over wax cappings melted down, you can assemble a relatively nice display for farmer's markets, beekeeper's associations, or other places to sell your honey.

**Figure 58: Honey Harvest Display**

# Chapter 7

## Winterizing Your Colony

Winter is a time of dormancy for a colony. How well the colony has gathered it's nectar stores during the nectar flow, and how well balanced the population of bees has been managed by the queen are two of the most significant factors for whether a colony will survive the winter dearth of nectar and pollen. However, there are some relatively simple measures a beekeeper can take to help the colony survive.

**1. Fall Feeding.** Probably one of the most important things you can do for your colony in the late summer and early fall is to feed your bees. There are actually two food items that are an essential part of this feeding: sugar syrup & pollen patties. As described in more detail in Chapter 5, section 1b, providing sugar syrup which has a lower ratio of water is an important step to take, especially for a new, or weak colony. This will help the colony store up the 30-40 lbs of honey they need to make it through the winter.

The second food item to provide in the fall period is supplemental pollen. This can be fed in a powder form in a common area, or in a patty form inside the hive. Pollen patties can be bought from a bee supplier, or made at home using a favorite pollen patty recipe. A recipe that I've used is found in Chapter 5, section 1a and in Appendix B.

Patties should be flattened enough so that they can be placed on top of the frames where the winter cluster will be located. A good place is just above the frames of the bottom brood chamber, and below the super frames above. Placing the patties in the very top of the super, below the inner cover, can often attract hive beetles, who seem to love the pollen patties as well.

**2. Winter Buttoning Up.**  Another important step that is helpful in ensuring the colony's survival is tightening up a bit on the open areas of the colony.  For example, closing up normally open areas such as the Varroa screen bottom boards can be helpful.  However, closing up a colony and providing "insulation" should be accomplished with great caution.  Wrapping or enclosing colonies with vapor proof barriers, such as blue poly laminate roof tarps, can lead to a disaster.

I've seen new beekeepers wrap or cover their colonies with blue poly tarps which later led to moisture entrapment.  Water entrapment during winter can be deadly to a colony of bees.  In the natural, bees use propolis to seal up their enclosed compartment, thereby managing and controlling the ventilation of the interior.  However, covering a colony with a tarp leads to the creation of a secondary high humidity climate outside the colony which the bees are completely unable to manage.  The high humidity is the opposite of the normally cold dry winter climate outside the hive that the bees are expecting.

Another way of visualizing this is the metaphor of a car parked outside running in the winter, in contrast with a car parked inside a garage running.  Like a colony of bees, the car parked outside is able to outgas exhaust into the wind which allows dissipation of noxious fumes, while the car parked inside ends up accumulating noxious fumes in the garage.  The bees need to be able to outgas carbon dioxide and humidity.  Enclosing a colony in the microclimate produced by a tarp will produce excessive amounts of moisture and carbon dioxide which can end up killing a colony.  Left to themselves the bees are able to exhaust $CO_2$ and humidity from inside the hive and take in ambient air from outside the colony.  Adding a tarp prevents them from being able to do that.

This is not to say the beekeeper cannot do anything helpful to winterize the colony.  There are a few simple steps you can take when buttoning up your colonies for winter.  First, change the entrance reducers from a larger opening to a smaller opening.  Second, close off screened Varroa boards using a foam insulation board, such as the ¾" blue insulation foam boards found in a building supply store. These will need to be cut and snugly fit in the board's opening.  Also, some type of clamp, duct tape or underlying varroa board will need to be used to keep the foam board from blowing off of the bottom of the hive. Winter winds can often pull off insulation boards if they are not well secured.

**Figure 59: Foam Board in Varroa Screen Bottom Board**

Finally, if you do chose to wrap your colonies, you will need to make sure that this is done snugly around the sides, without blocking the upper and lower ventilation ports.  In the past, I have used roofers felt, and silver bubble-wrap insulation to wrap colonies.  Both work well as long as adequate ventilation is preserved.

Another final way of providing feed and at the same time helping the bees with moisture management is through the use of candy boards.  The basic construction of a candy board involves a slightly deeper inner cover, in which the ¼ to ½ inch space is used to pour a layer of sugar candy.  If properly prepared, the bees will be able to feed from the surface of this board inside the colony as moisture provides an edible candy syrup.  Plans and recipe for a simple candy board can be found in Appendix C.

**3.  Early Spring Feeding.** As spring approaches, winter stores will have been significantly drawn down.  In some parts of the country you can get a certain amount of warming, while the spring nectar flow is still weeks away.   If bees come out of cluster during this time, they will be consuming more honey stores than in the colder cluster state.  For this reason it's important to check your colony's honey stores and consider feeding if needed.

One simple way to check your colony's level of honey stores without opening or disturbing your colony is to gently lift the back of the colony.  The average person can usually lift 40 lbs without a lot of effort.  When you're lifting the back of the colony, the front of your stand is taking about half of the load of the colony, while you are lifting the other half of the total weight.  (Please exercise caution when  you do this so that you don't tip the hive over.)

If you're feeling about 20 lbs of weight on the back side, your colony is currently weighing about 40 lbs.  This is probably the minimum weight you would want for your colony toward the end of winter.  If the colony has gotten this light, it is time to provide 2:1 sugar syrup, a candy board, a pollen patty, or a combination of all the above.  Providing pollen patties in late winter can also help to stimulate brood build up.  This will help to build a strong colony population that will be available for the spring nectar flow.

If you find that your colony is extremely light, providing regular granulated sugar on the top of the inner cover is a quick way of performing emergency winter feeding without opening the colony to outside cold weather.  When you find a colony that is exceedingly light, another check that you can do to confirm that your colony is still alive is to first, place your ear to the back of the colony.  Gently knock with your knuckle against the side of the colony and see if you hear a buzzing hum.  This hum will surge and then die back down if your colony is alive.  Guard bees will likely emerge from the entrance as well.   If you don't hear a response, you'll probably want to open and check for a dead out condition.  If that's the case, removing the honeycomb frames to a freezer to protect the valuable comb from wax moth destruction is advisable.  Those frames can then be provided to another colony later if there are no signs of disease or pests.

If you're of average strength and cannot lift the back of the colony, most likely you're feeling at least 50 lbs of weight and the colony has a total weight of about 100 lbs.  Remember, this total weight does include the weight of the wooden frames and hive boxes.  If you can't easily lift the back of your colony, this is a good indication that your colony has sufficient honey stores, and is likely a strong colony.  It's a good idea to check your colonies for weight on a monthly basis.  This will help you to identify colonies needing emergency winter feeding.

One final word on winterizing your colony - as you begin to approach the months when the outdoor temperatures will drop well below 40° F it's important to remove any queen excluders from the colony.  During the winter months, the colony will exist as a tight cluster somewhere within the hive.  This cluster will move around the colony over the honey stores.

Once the honey stores are depleted in the area around the brood chamber, the winter colony will naturally move up into the supers.  If there is a queen excluder left over the brood chamber, this can isolate the swarm from the queen and lead to the death of the queen and the eventual collapse of the colony.  For this reason, if you use queen excluders make certain to remove them in the fall before winter sets in.  This will help promote the growth of a much healthier colony in the spring.

# Chapter 8

## How to Grow Your Apiary

As mentioned earlier in Chapter 3, there are five basic you ways you can acquire bees in order to expand or grow your apiary: ordering package bees, ordering a nuclear colony, purchasing a full hive, collecting a swarm, or trapping out a colony. However, once you've gotten your first two or three colonies going, and you've learned to manage the health of your bees, there is another source that you now have which can easily be used to create new colonies. This method employs the natural reproductive ability of a colony to produce a new colony by way of a "hive split."

There are a number of different techniques you can use to create a split, which can be found in a simple search of articles and videos on the internet. However, there are three basic methods I've found that are simple and work well. The first is a hive split built upon a purchased queen, the second is a hive split built upon a queen cell, and the third is a hive split produced by a split produced queen. These are in order, starting with the simplest method.

**Figure 61: Queen Cell**
(Photo by Mike Bright)

In all three of these techniques you are producing what's referred to as a "nuclear colony",  also called a nuc.  One of the tools used in producing a nuclear colony is what's called a nuc box.  This is a mini, 5-frame brood chamber, which allows the nuclear colony to start off in a smaller chamber that will be easier for the colony to defend and keep thermally managed.  Although there are many different nuc designs that beekeepers use, in the figure below I've shown three different types of nuc boxes, with four different types of feeding arrangements.

The first on the left is a very economical nuc box design, manufactured by Kevin Jester.  Jester Bees was my first bee source supplier after I got back into beekeeping.  The

**Figure 62: Different Nuclear Colony Set-Ups**

advantages of the Jester nuc box is that it's lightweight and economical in cost due to it's being cleverly constructed with corrugated plastic board. If you're working with a larger number of nucs, the light weight Jester Nuc is particularly helpful, and the plastic lasts a lot longer than similar nucs made of wax-coated corrugated cardboard. The feeding method depicted for this nuc is a homemade feeder made from a 1 quart restaurant take-out container. Drilling about 30 very tiny holes in the lid of this container will allow the bees to come up through a ¾ in drilled hole in the lid of the nuc, and access the sugar syrup in the small crawl space under the inverted lid.

The next nuc from the left is a nuc box that I purchased from a supplier. However, on this nuc and the far right nuc shown open (same size), I built the tops and bottoms. The second nuc uses a 16-ounce plastic drink bottle with small holes drilled in the lid, which is then inverted and placed in a matching hole in the wooden lid of the nuc box. The fourth nuc, with lid removed, shows a 4-frame and single frame feeder arrangement.

The third nuc is a more expensive cypress nuc, with telescoping lid and inner cover. This nuc shows the use of the Boardman feeder. The one drawback of the Boardman feeder is that the close access to the entrance can often attract robbing from other colonies. Feeding in ways similar to the other three arrangements places the access to the syrup deeper in the colony, and thus less accessible to outside robbing bees. Once you've decided on a particular nuc to use, you can choose one of the three methods to start your new nuclear colony.

**1. Purchased Queen Hive Split.** If you find a queen producer who provides good quality queens for your area, you can use your existing spring colonies to produce new nuclear colonies. The things you will need to start your split are a queen, two frames of brood, a frame with some pollen, a frame of honey, and an empty frame.  The greatest challenge to this method will be getting a supplied queen early enough in the spring to capitalize on your colony's spring build-up of brood and bees.

Once you provide the necessary queen, two frames of brood, a frame of pollen, and a frame of honey, you can go ahead and place these 4 frames in a nuc box, along with the additional frame, or feeder, depending on your feeding arrangement.  It's essential to provide either a frame feeder or top feeder to help the colony produce the wax necessary for drawing out the empty frames.  One cautionary note: make sure that you don't accidentally include the queen from your parent colony in your newly started colony.  If that happens, when the new queen is released from her queen cage, there will be a fight to the death, ending with only one of your two queens left.

It's also a good idea to shake a frame or two of young nurse bees from a frame of brood into your new colony, again making sure not to include the old queen.  This will provide a healthy number of bees for your new population.  Once this is done, place the queen cage in between two frames near the top with the cage's cork or stopper removed. This is so the bees can chew away the sugar fondant, and release the queen once the colony has grown accustomed to her pheromone scent.  You'll need to check after 3 days to make sure the queen has been released.

One of the problems in releasing a queen to a colony is that the release door/tube can sometimes become clogged with a dead attendant bee.  Placing the cage with the release hole in the upward direction will prevent this from happening. (See Figures 31 & 63).  If you find that after three days the bees for some reason have not been able to eat through the candy

blockage, go ahead and remove the candy, or open the other
entrance. The queen
and attendants should
then exit down into
their new home. If
you're introducing a
queen during a very hot
period, be careful not
to place the queen cage
too high in the nuc or
brood chamber.
Otherwise, she could
overheat and die. This
can be particularly true
with corrugated plastic
nucs, where there's not
much insulation
between the top and
the frames.

**Figure 63: Queen Cage
Placement**

Once your queen has been released, it's important to check
and make sure your new queen is healthy and laying brood. A
failed queen can lead to the death of a colony if the problem is
not caught. After your queen has begun to lay eggs and
produce brood, your new colony is on its way to becoming a
productive member of your growing apiary.

After assembling your four nuclear frames from the parent
colony in your nuc, adding an additional frame and queen cell
you'll need to make certain that the new colony is at least 3
miles away from the parent colony. This is so that the worker
bees do not return to the old parent colony, depleting the
colony's population in the process. You'll probably want to
wait to add the sugar syrup to the feeder until you've moved
the nuc to its new location to prevent sloshing of the syrup.

Add the syrup immediately after moving the nuc, because the new colony will need a food source right away.  It might be a good idea to add the queen cage at the other end as well.

Another method that I've found is useful in disorienting a new colony from their old location, is to put the new colony on lock-down in a fairly dark cool (65°F) area, like a shed.  This can also be done in the originating apiary if it's cool enough.  It's important to use a moving screen or other means of confinement to make certain the bees don't get out and return to the old colony.  It's also important to provide feed and good ventilation during this time.  After three days you can move the new nuclear colony to your original apiary and most of the bees will no longer be triangulated to their former location.

**2.  Queen Cell Hive Split.**  Another great way to produce a new colony is by the use of a queen cell.  Some queen producers sell queen cells at a cheaper rate than a caged producing queen.  However, if you have a successful stock of bees that you have found to be docile and hygienic in their character traits, you may want to watch for that colony's production of queen cells during spring or times of swarming.

When you find a queen cell that you'd like to graft into a nuclear colony, go ahead and prepare a nuclear colony using the same method described above in the Purchased Queen Hive Split method.  Once the new frames are prepared, carefully remove the peanut shaped queen cell from the parent colony by cutting at the support base of the cell.  Be careful not to cut into the chamber of the queen when you do this.  You may even want to sacrifice any brood cells around the queen cell in order not to disturb or injure the developing queen.

Treat the queen cell as you would any delicate creature, knowing that a careless bump or squeeze could cripple and maim the new queen as she develops.  Like the queen cage, the cell should be placed in the top section of a frame.  You can press the base of the cell into a section of capped honey, making sure the other adjacent frame face has capped brood. This will ensure that the queen cell is cared for by the nurse bees.  After you've done this and closed up the new colony, the colony should be left alone for at least 7 days.

Another simple method that does not involve grafting the queen cell is to find a frame that has a queen cell, and use that as one of your four nuclear frames.  Once the nuclear colony is assembled, it will take at least a couple of weeks after the queen has emerged before she will have mated and begun to produce brood. Once you see brood, your colony is now a functioning colony, and after a few more weeks you can taper off on the supplemental sugar syrup feeding.  Be sure to add additional frames or supers as the bees build, otherwise your nuclear colony may become overcrowded by honey and brood, and your new colony may begin the swarming process.

**3.  Hive Split Produced Queen.**  Although there are a variety of ways that beekeepers have found to produce splits, the third and final simple method I have found productive is to allow the nuclear colony to produce its own queen cell.  This does present some risk, since it is not always successful. However, paying close attention to providing the right elements for producing a queen will enhance the successful production of a queen right colony.  A queen right colony is a colony that has a healthy laying queen.

To begin the hive split produced queen, prepare the 4 frame nuclear colony using the same method described in the Purchased Queen Hive Split method.  However, in this method it's very important to ensure that one of your brood frames has larvae or egg cells that are no more than 3

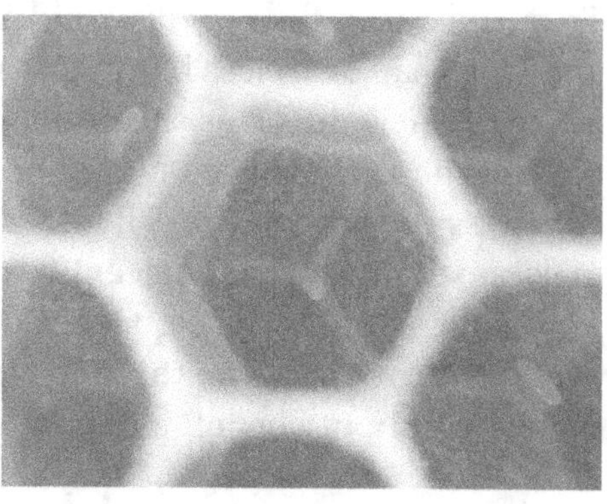

**Figure 64: Cells with Egg**

days old.  Newly laid eggs can be identified by their appearance; they look like a tiny grain of rice, standing up from one end in the bottom of the cell.  As the egg hatches into a larva the nurse bees will provide tiny amounts of royal jelly to feed the larva. At first the larva will appear like a small white comma down in the bottom of the cell.

**Figure 65: Cells with Inverted Queen Cup**

When you find an egg cell, carefully trim away several cells beneath the egg cell, keeping the egg's cell intact.  This is in order to allow the worker bees to form a peanut shaped queen cell out and down from the egg cell.  Some beekeepers use the end of the hive tool to smash the cells beneath as a recess for queen cell formation.

Make sure to have pollen and honey facing the egg on the next adjacent frame, directly across from your future queen's egg cell.  The closer you can get your pollen and honey to the specially configured egg cell, the better environment there will be for the efficient production of a new queen. Finding a queen cup is an even better environment. The emergency "queen cup" is a feature that colonies usually build in case of the death of a queen.  This is bulbous shaped cell that is about 5/8 inches in diameter, and often stands out on the surface of the comb.  Colonies will then use this to develop a new queen cell.

Finding a peanut-shaped capped queen cell is even better than finding a queen cup, because it means that the colony has already produced a new queen which could emerge anytime in the next seven days (See Figure 61).  The one drawback is that during the first few days after being capped, the queen cell is very delicate and could be damaged if the cell is jostled and the larvae becomes detached from the top of the cell.  So, take great care when working with the queen cell.

The other important thing to remember in good queen development is that your new queen will require a copious amount of royal jelly.  The better your nuclear colony accomplishes this, the healthier and more productive your new queen will be.  Consequently, it's important to provide sugar syrup during the first two weeks of your nuclear colony and ensure that a frame with pollen is available.  The typical development time for a new queen is 14 days.  After that, the virgin queen will emerge and, within the next 7-10 days, will go on her mating flight.  For this reason, it's important to time the creation of your nuclear colony when temperatures will be above 60°F, drones will be available,  it is not too windy, and skies will be clear enough for the mating flight. This varies in different parts of the world.  High winds can be particularly problematic for mating flights.

When using this method, it's important not to disturb the frames or colony for at least 10 days after the hive split.  On day 10, the cell has reached the pupa stage and is not as vulnerable to movement of the frames.  However, moving the frames or colony before this time can result in injury to the larva, which can potentially deform the new queen.

Once you've verified on approximately Day 10 of development that the queen cell has been constructed, you're on your way to a successful hive split.  If no cell is apparent on Day 10, try to provide another frame with eggs to try and produce a queen.  If there is still no queen cell produced after the second try, recombine frames with another weak colony through the use of a newspaper barrier placed over the top of the parent colony and the added frames above the newspaper barrier.  This is to prevent the failed split from developing "laying workers", which will end up creating a weak queen-less-colony that cannot reproduce, and that will eventually die without a fertile queen.

When you find that your colony has produced a new queen cell, check again at Day 21 to ensure that you have a laying queen. If there are no eggs or larvae present then, check again in a week to verify that you have a laying queen with a consistent brood pattern.  Once you see that your new queen has begun creating a good and healthy brood pattern, you now have a successful hive split.  See Figure 66 for an example of a healthy brood pattern.

**Figure 66: Healthy Brood Pattern**

# Chapter 9

## Treating Common Problems

Over the last 40 years, there has been an increase in the number of scourges that have put pressure on the bee population in the world.  Here in the United States we've always seen the problem of wax moths and American foulbrood.  However, since the early 1970's we've seen an increase of other scourges including Africanized bees, Israeli bee virus, varroa mites, tracheal mites, small hive beetles, and colony collapse disorder.

### 1.  Neonicotinoids & Fungicides.

In 2006, the sudden disappearance of colonies of bees left beekeepers wondering what was happening to the bee population.  This became known as colony collapse disorder.  Most experts believe this can be attributed to the rise of both an increase in fungicidal use on crops, as well as the use of a new group of insecticides known as neonicotinoids.

In their inception, neonicotinoids were thought to be less toxic to mammals and birds than traditional pesticides, and were originally only supposed to affect chewing insects that parasitically invade crops like corn.  According to manufacturers of this family of insecticides, by the time the corn went to tassel, the half-life of the neonicotinoids had reduced their concentration to virtually zero.  However, what many did not consider was that when the neonicotinoid is coated on seed corn and seeds are sown, the dust from the seeds could travel to nearby colonies of bees and wipe out entire colonies.  Of course, some might claim that the same thing can happen when crop dusters and application of traditional pesticides are broadcast, and similar results can and do occur.

In coping with the existence of pesticides, fungicides and neonicotinoids, what is the average beekeeper to do?  One measure might be to totally avoid apiary locations near farms where pesticide treatment can be expected.  Another less severe, yet challenging approach, would be to contact local farmers near where you keep bees and make sure to find out when they are treating their crops.  The beekeeper can then make sure to close up the colonies during those periods.

To prevent colonies from exposure to known pesticide treatments, colonies can be closed up by either blocking entrances or placing moving screens.  The entrance can be closed off the night before a treatment is to occur and opened a day or two later.  Through the use of moving screens on your colony, you can allow ventilation, but prevent your bees from travelling to nearby fields when conditions are adverse. This could also include periods of spraying for mosquitoes.

**2. Small Hive Beetles.**  As mentioned earlier in Chapter 5, small hive beetles, or SHB can often be kept to a low level by locating colonies that have full sun in the day but shade in the late afternoon.  This appears to be a strong deterrent against SHB.  However, another non-toxic way of dealing with SHB is by placing SHB traps in your hive.  These traps usually have a small or large reservoir that can be filled

**Figure 67: Small Hive Beetle**

with vegetable oil.  There are a variety of traps that are placed in between the tops of frames, and others that are placed below a bottom board.  Most make use of vegetable oil that acts as a deadly trap to the SHB when they attempt to flee from the worker bees.  Strips of apple, or a drop or two of vinegar seems to make the oil bath attractive to beetles.

Some varieties of bees are much more aggressive about fighting against SHB, while other bees appear more docile toward their adversaries.  Another means of combating and coping with the existence of SHB, is by choosing a good line of queens that are more hygienic and more SHB resistant. These are queens that have been specially bred to be behaviorally prone to cleaning and SHB chasing. In addition, there are other non-organic means of treating for SHB. However, those means will not be discussed here, and can usually be found on the internet or in bee supplier catalogs if you choose to pursue that route.

**3. Tracheal Mites.**  Another recent source of colony attrition among the bee population has been due to the scourge of tracheal mites, also known under the scientific name *Acarapis Woodi*.  Unlike varroa mites, tracheal mites actually invade the internal respiratory system of the bee.  These microscopic mites end up becoming so numerous inside an infected bee that they actually clog the trachea or breathing tube of the bees, thus the name tracheal mites.  This tracheal invasion results in a lack of oxygen and a very weakened and unhealthy bee.

Although dissection and microscopic examination is required in order to completely diagnose tracheal mites, this disease, also known as Acarine Disease, can also be diagnosed by a few symptoms that typically are seen in tracheal mite infestations. One of the first symptoms can be recognized at the entrance of a colony is the noticeable inability to fly.  Imagine if you had to run a race, breathing through a straw.  That's essentially what happens to the bee and it incapacitates them so they cannot fly.

When an infected colony suddenly has a significant percentage of the population that cannot fly, there are certain things that will inevitably happen.  The inability to fly leads to a shorter lifespan and a degradation of honey stores due to the lack of workers.  The weakened ability for oxygen exchange can lead to shortened life spans of worker bees, and the colony can quickly collapse into just a small cluster of bees and a queen, even though it still has honey stores.  The smaller the cluster becomes, the less they are able to maintain a warm temperature core for the queen.  If you find these conditions evident after a winter, this could be evidence that you have colonies affected with tracheal mites.  The other symptom is the appearance of akimbo or out-of-position wings.  However, the out-of-position wings could also be evidence of a bee virus that usually follows with Varroa mites as well.  Varroa mites are known to be carrier of bee viruses During winter, when a colony is in a tight cluster, the spread of tracheal mites can become rampant.

If you suspect tracheal mites, another more precise method of diagnosis is to collect several bees with the akimbo wings, which are then placed in a small jar containing one inch of isopropyl alcohol to preserve them.  They can then be sent to your state's Cooperative Extension office or state bee inspector's office, which are usually located at or associated with one of the major agricultural universities.  Ironically, this service is becoming more and more difficult to find with the spread of Africanized honeybees throughout the continental United States.

One of the ways of treating for tracheal mites is by providing either menthol pellets or a paper towel that has a small amount of menthol essential oil.  The bees will chew away the menthol laced paper towel, and in doing so will rid themselves of the tracheal mites.  Make sure honey supers are removed before using menthol products to avoid tainting the flavor of the honey.  Some have found that products like Honey Bee Healthy, which contains essential oils, are effective in the control of tracheal mites and some bee viruses.  When dealing with essential oils, it's important to be very careful, because the concentrated essential oils can be toxic to small children and sometimes even adults.

**4.  Varroa Mites.**  There are a few things you'll need to regularly do to ensure that your colony is not infected with Varroa mites.  As discussed earlier in Chapters 1 & 2,  an important step for today's hive is the use of bottom boards with a Varroa screen bottom board, instead of the traditional solid bottom board.  The Varroa screen board is a bottom board that is somewhat like a picture frame with most of the surface area of the bottom replaced with a 1/8" by 1/8" wirecloth

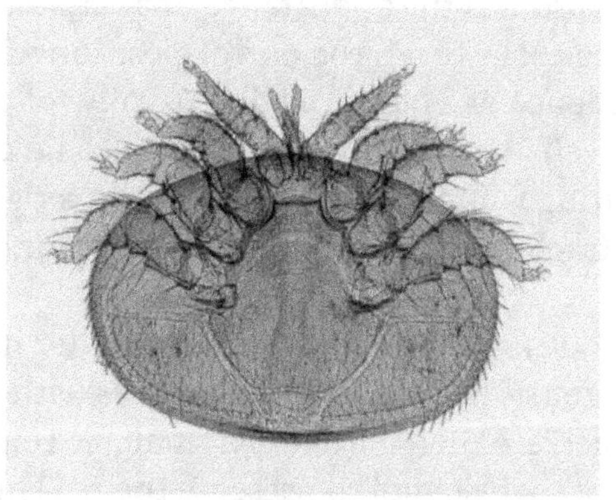

**Figure 68 Varroa Destructor**

screen (See Figure 19).  When used in conjunction with a powdered sugar shake (See figure 42 and Pages 59-60), the powdered sugar facilitates varroa mites being groomed off of the bees to drop through the screen and down to the ground rather than being able to be caught by the bottom board and crawl back up.

One quick way to check for Varroa mites is to remove a couple of drone pupae from their capped cells. Another way to check for the presence of Varroa mites is to place about 4 tablespoons of powdered sugar in a quart mason jar. Prior to adding bees, a small 1/8" x 1/8" wire screen is cut into the same size as the circular jar top insert. This is then placed on the inside of the Mason jar lid ring. Next, a half cup scoop of bees is dumped into the jar, and the lid is closed with the specially prepared screen top. The mason jar is then shaken vigorously over a sheet of legal sized or 11 x 14 white paper. The bees are then released, and the rest of the sugar is dumped on the paper. Using a magnifying glass, carefully check for the presence of Varroa mites. These will appear as a reddish brown dot about the size of the dot at the

end of this sentence.· If you find more than about 12 Varroa mites, you should treat using one of the following means:

**a. Sugar Dowsing.** One means of treatment is by dowsing frames with powdered sugar, either by way of a sugar shaker as described above, or by being

**Figure 69: Sugar Dusting for Varroa Mites**

puffed into the chamber via a specially designed bellows tool as shown in Figure 69. This is a fairly good preventative treatment, which will help knock off a large number of Varroa mites. This primarily occurs by way of the grooming action of bees who are licking the powdered sugar off of their fellow bees. You'll need to check your mite count in two weeks to see if the population has been reduced.

This technique is most effective when coupled with the Varroa screen bottom board. Otherwise, with a solid bottom, the mites will simply crawl back up after being knocked down to the bottom board.

**Figure 70: Placement of Thymol with ¾ in Shim**

**b. Thymol.** Another slightly more aggressive form of treatment for Varroa mites is by way of a natural treatment product that uses a sublimating gel base containing essential oils from the thyme plant. You'll need to make sure that you have temperatures above 70°F, but hopefully well below 100°F when you do this treatment. You'll also want to make sure you don't have honey supers on that you plan on extracting soon after.  The Thymol will leave a mouthwash-tasting thyme flavor in your honey if you do.

Make sure to carefully follow the instructions on the Thymol product labeling.  This usually requires the use of a ¾ to 1 in shim, as shown in Figure 70.  This is to provide a slightly larger space over the frames to accommodate the sublimating Thymol foil can.  The method also usually requires two successive treatments to eliminate the Varroa mite life cycle. Once you've done this, the sugar shake count should reveal whether you've eliminated Varroa mites from your colony.

For more extensive information on controlling Varroa mites, there's a really great online resource entitled "Tools for Varroa Management" by the Honey Bee Health Organization.  This can be downloaded in PDF form and includes several additional techniques for Varroa mite control.

**5.  Israeli Bee Virus & Other Viruses**.  Altogether, there are about 24 different viruses that are affecting bee populations around the world.  In the last several years there have been a number of emerging bee viruses that have been linked to colony collapse disorder and rapid bee die off.  One such virus is known as the Israeli bee virus, technically named the Israeli acute paralysis virus (IAPV).  This is a serious bee virus which affects the bee at the genetic or mitochondrial level of the bee's cellular organs.  IAPV can infect colonies even when there is no appearance of symptoms.  Studies showed that IAPV is one of the third most common bee viruses.

Although there are about twenty-four different viruses that the bee population is currently fighting, one of the most effective ways of promoting health and combating bee viruses is through the use of vitamin enriched and essential oil supplements. One of the feeding supplements I've found to be helpful in promoting bee health and staving off viruses is Honey Bee Healthy.  This is a supplement which includes, sugar, water, lecithin, spearmint, and lemongrass oils.

Honey Bee Healthy or similar essential oil products can be added to pollen patties, sugar syrup feed, and sugar water sprays.  Whenever I notice a colony that appears to be a little less energetic than the other colonies or has any sign of deformed wings in young bees or pupae, I spray a weak solution using one of the essential oil supplements and l usually supplement with sugar syrup feeding as well.  Usually the weak colony will respond within a few weeks of this feed supplement treatment.  If the colony continues to be weak after a second treatment, it may be advisable to requeen.

**6. Africanized Bees.**  Another one of the scourges that has beset the beekeeper is the introduction and intrusion of the Africanized bee into North America.  Africanized honey bees (AHB), were actually introduced into Brazil by entomologists back in the 1950's. European honey bees, EHB (Apis mellifera) were cross bred with African honeybees (Apis mellifera scutellata).  The Brazillian bee experiments were an attempt to increase honey production using the genetic traits of the Africanized bees.  During these experiments, several swarms escaped into the jungles of South America and began working their way up into North America.  Back in the 1970's, I recall hearing of concerns with Africanized bees in South Florida. However, it wasn't until the early 1990's that Africanized bees became an official invasive species in South Texas.

According to the Texas Apiary Inspection Service, Africanized bees will tend to choose lower ground dwellings such as water meter boxes, swarm more abundantly than EHB and exhibit more aggressive and defensive behaviors.  Whereas a typical

EHB colony sends out ten guard bees to ward off intruders, an AHB colony will send out more than 100 guard bees. Africanized colonies will also pursue their adversaries farther than 100 yards from the colony, whereas an EHB colony will typically pursue an intruder no more than 50 yards from the colony.

Although it is almost impossible to distinguish AHB from EHB, positive identification can be made by specialized test facilities. This can be done by morphological examination of the size of bee body parts such as the lengths of legs and wings. Genetic testing of bees is also another means of positively identifying AHB. Over the last few years AHB has become so widespread in Texas that quarantines have become ineffective.

As a beekeeper, it is important to be aware of the local laws concerning Africanized honey bees. The other important thing a beekeeper needs to be aware of is how a colony can become Africanized. When a colony re-queens, in some areas there are enough Africanized drones that the mating of a queen ends up producing Africanized stock. Consequently, one way to combat Africanized bees in your area is through regular re-queening. To be relatively certain of non-AHB stock, queens can be acquired from a state certified queen breeder.

Still, even European Honeybees can demonstrate defensive behavior when they are provoked. There have been cases where horses and domestic animals have been killed by large colonies of European honey bees when the bees were threatened or provoked by the animals. Colonies can also become "hot" in temperament if they are experiencing predators such as skunks. If you find scratch marks on the front of your hive box, and balls of chewed up bees on the ground in front of your colony, you are very likely experiencing night time attrition by a skunk. This colony will also likely exhibit defensive behavior similar to the defensive response seen in Africanized bees.

If, over time, you continue to experience persistent aggressive behavior by one of your colonies you likely have an Africanized colony. Africanized behavior includes being chased more than 100 yards by 25 or more bees. Another indicator is the presence of significantly more brood than honey production. If you notice these behaviors and suspect the possibility of AHB influence, it is highly recommended that you re-queen.

The first measure in dealing with Africanized colonies is to move them away from humans and animals. You should transport your colony to a more remote and safe location while replacing the queen in order to ensure human and animal safety until the colony can be passivated and rid of the AHB aggressive genetic stock. Extremely aggressive colonies of AHB should be euthanized. It's also very important for new beekeepers to consult a more experienced beekeeper and possibly your state or local bee inspector for how to respond to AHB or suspected AHB in your area.

**7. American Foulbrood.** American foulbrood is caused by *Paenibacillus larvae,* an infectious bacterium which not only can wipe out a colony, but can also destroy your apiary and feral bee colonies in your area as well. This bacterial infection is started when spores from an infected colony are brought in either through a contaminated food source or from a bee who has participated in robbing from another colony that has been infected with the AFB *Paenibacillus larvae* bacteria spores.

American foulbrood will infect bee larvae that are exposed to AFB spores. Most often the infected larvae will die and rot in the capped cells. This usually results in capped brood cells that have a sunken and sometimes moist appearance. These cells are typically slightly darker in appearance and will usually have a noxious odor. This is the reason for the name foul brood. Infected larvae often appear a sickly yellowish color.

There are cases where AFB is present, but the foul smell is not noticed. Another classic symptom can be found in infected colonies by pricking open the sunken brood cells. If the larvae appear to be dead, with a caramel colored or light brown appearance, this may be a strong indicator that your colony is infected with AFB. Another old school test is to take a toothpick or match stick, and pluck out the dead larvae. If the larva has a viscous consistency with an elastic spring-back like a rubber band, then most likely your colony has been infected with AFB. Sparse brood patterns, where the bees have cleared out dead larvae may also be a symptom of AFB.

In the not too distant past, mild cases of AFB were treated with the antibiotic, Terramycin. However, as of 2015, the Federal laws have changed and purchase of this antibiotic now requires a veterinarian prescription. Consequently, if your colony is suspected of having AFB or of having been exposed to AFB, you should consult either a more experienced beekeeper or your state bee inspector. Your local beekeeping club may be able to help you with this. The bee inspector can give professional guidance on what measures to take and can issue a prescription if deemed appropriate. In the case of AFB, destruction of the colony and equipment might be required.

It is very important to research and study the laws concerning AFB in your particular state.  Some states require the burning of all woodenware, brood, and bees that have become infected with AFB.  This is because AFB spores can last up to 40 years in a dry or desiccated condition.  Even in states which do not require burning, it may be advisable to isolate and burn a badly affected colony.  This is especially true if you have a large number of colonies in a particular location where the disease could quickly spread.

In Europe, beekeepers whose colonies become infected with European foulbrood, caused by the bacterium *Melissococcus plutonius,* are required to euthanize the bees and then destroy their infected apiary by burning and burying the bees and equipment.  As mentioned previously, if you're a new beekeeper, it's advisable to contact a more experienced beekeeper or local beekeeping club if you suspect you have a colony that is infected with AFB.

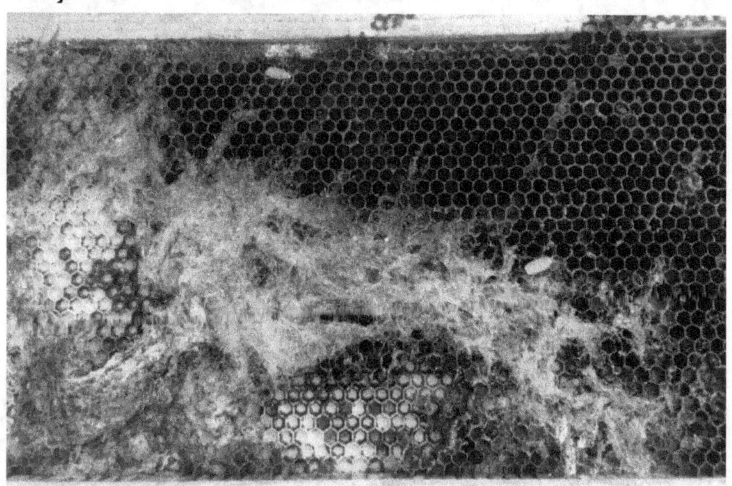

**Figure 71: Wax Moth Damage with Spidery Web**

**8. Wax Moths.** Wax moths have been a pest to beekeepers for a number of decades. However, the greater and lesser wax moths are actually a natural part of the Lord's clean-up crew and are tasked with cleaning up the wax remnants of weakened or dead colonies. The wax moth will invade a weakened colony and produce a mass of spider web like fibers, as they reduce the wax honeycomb and food stores to a powdery black residue.

**Figure 72: Wooden Frame Wax Moth Damage**

The appearance of wax moths in a beekeeper's weak or dying colony is a heart-wrenching sight. In fact, not only do wax moths destroy the valuable wax honeycomb in a colony, they will also destroy expensive woodenware such as frames and hive bodies. They do this through the chewing of gouges and holes for the nesting of their larvae, as they begin the metamorphosis from larvae, to pupae, to winged moth.

Over the years, I've found that the best way to combat wax moths is to promote healthy colonies that can stave off wax moth invasion, since the bees will usually successfully defend their colonies against the moths if the colonies are healthy. When the bees are not present, the beekeeper must protect his assets against wax moth destruction by being careful about the storage of uninhabited honeycomb. Honeycomb stored without bees is a written invitation for wax moth larvae, or small hive beetle larvae. Once you have wax moths reproducing in your area, you can end up with a veritable air force of moths that your bees will have to defend against.

**Figure 73: Wax Moth Larva**

Oftentimes, the wax moth, or SHB have been in a colony and left their eggs before being dispatched by a strong colony. These eggs are usually either cleaned up, or caught at the early small larvae phase by the bees. This typically happens before the larvae can do damage. However, removing honeycomb from the bees can oftentimes

**Figure 74: Wax Moth Cocoon**

end up in a hatch out of existing eggs which then becomes a
growing infestation without the combative strength of a
healthy colony.

Some beekeepers resort to the use of wax moth crystals
during the storage of empty supers during winter months.
However, one of the active ingredients of wax moth crystals is
para-dichlorobenzene.  Although beekeepers for decades have
used moth crystals, chlorinated hydrocarbons, and especially
benzene ring molecules have been scientifically proven to
cause cancer.  Benzene ring molecules like these are no longer
used as solvents in organic chemistry classes due to their
known carcinogenic effects.  For this reason, I highly
recommend steering clear of the use of any wax moth crystals
in beekeeping.  A better approach is to leave empty supers on
a strong colony during winter months.  The bees will keep the
honeycomb protected much better than would moth crystals.

**9.  Queenless Colony or Laying Workers.** Another basic
challenge that the beekeepers face is what's referred to as a
queenless colony.  This condition can lead to the
development of "laying workers."  Whenever a colony
becomes queenless, the worker and nurse bees have about 72
hours to respond to the crisis which could lead to the
eventual death of the colony.

After having 72 hours of no queen, or no production of queen
cell, there will no longer be eggs available for the full
development of a queen.  In the absence of the queen
pheromone, some worker bees will develop the ability to lay
eggs.  However, these eggs are infertile, and will only result in
drone brood.

There are several symptoms of a laying worker colony.  The
first symptom is the obvious symptom of a missing queen.  In

addition, if the queenless condition continues the colony's behavior will change, since it will be acting without the presence of the queen's ordering pheromone.  Colonies at this state will begin to exhibit comb gnawing and distorted construction of the honeycomb structure.  The bees behavior will lead to a colony that looks like it is on some kind of terrible mind-altering drug.  The comb will no longer have the nice geometric pattern typical of the beautiful of bee architecture. Instead, the patterns will be irregular and distorted.

Some of the worker bees will develop their own ability to lay eggs; however, those eggs will be unfertilized and will therefore lead to the production of drone brood only.  Laying workers will also lay multiple eggs in one cell.  Although this sometimes happens with new queens, this is probably the most tell-tale sign of the presence of laying workers.

The other problem with laying workers is that each laying worker will emit just enough pheromone in her partially fertile state to produce for herself a gang of attending worker bees that will treat her like a queen.  These attendants will fight off other contending queens or workers.  Consequently, before introducing a new queen, the colony  first must be purged of the laying workers.  This can be done by taking the entire colony about 50-75 yards from the old location.  Shake out all of the bees, and then return the empty hive back to its' original location.  The normal workers will return to the hive, but the laying worker will be left at the dumping site, unable to fly back to the old colony.  A new queen can then be introduced or the weakened queenless colony can be added to another weak colony as described below.

**10. Weak Colony.**  If you find at the end of a season going into fall that you have a weak colony, or colonies, the best thing that you can do to preserve the valuable wax and hardware is to merge the colony with another weak colony or with a stronger colony.  In order to do this, you must first kill the weaker queen.  Once this is done, you can remove the bottom of the hive and place the weak colony on the top of the other colony.

In order to gradually acclimatize the two colonies to one another, a sheet of newspaper is placed between the two colonies.  This allows the pheromone and scent of the queen to intermingle with the new merging colony.  As this happens the bees will gradually chew away the newspaper barrier, until the two colonies are merged into one. Once this is done, the colony and equipment are now in a better position to weather the winter together.

**Figure 75: Swarm 2009 - The Beginning**

# Chapter 10

# Closing Thoughts

In this handbook, I've attempted to equip you with all the basics that you need to get started in beekeeping. In **"Equipment Basics,"** my intent was to help you know the essential tools of beekeeping. **"Basic Bee Life and Nomenclature"** was to educate you on bee behavior, and fundamentals of the lifecycle of a bee. The third chapter, **"Simple Ways to Acquire the Colony"**, was to not only give ideas for meeting the difficult challenge of acquiring bees, but also to help you minimize the possibility of colony loss.

Knowing the **"Basics for Setting up a Hive"** is the next logical step in getting ready for your bees, so this was included in chapter 4. Once you've set up a bee hive, and populated it with bees, the next logical step is **"Maintaining a Healthy Colony."** This was provided to help you face the modern challenges of keeping bees alive in healthy in an increasingly difficult environment. Of course, one of the great benefits of raising bees is **"Harvesting Honey Stores"**, but even that can be challenging, and if it's not done properly can lead to the weakening and loss of your bees.

Another important factor in keeping your bees healthy over the long haul is the practice of **"Winterizing Your Colony"**. Although I wrote this book primarily targeting Southern environments, like Texas, Arkansas, Louisiana, Mississippi, Alabama, Georgia and Florida, the principles can be applied all the way to remote locations like Alaska and Hawaii.

Once you've become an established beekeeper with a small apiary, you can use the instructions on "**How to Grow Your Apiary**." This should help coach you on basic procedures which will eventually enable you to reproduce your own nuclear colonies. Also, in "**Treating Common Problems**" I provided a list of typical problems, and corresponding solutions that should hopefully help you cope with some of the health problems beekeepers face. Finally, under **References**, I've given you a list of helpful manuals and texts that I've used over the years to educate myself on beekeeping.

In his book on "Five Acres and Independence", Maurice G. Kains quotes the famous entomologist and beekeeper J. H. Comstock as saying "any many who can make $1,500 out of bees has ability to make at least $2,000 out of something else!" The take away is that beekeeping is known to many as one of the most difficult of farming, requiring a great deal of attention to detail, hard work and dedication. In order to do well, you'll need to study and work hard at it.

There's a lot of information out on the internet on beekeeping that is very helpful. However, at the same time, there is a good bit of mis-information out there as well. Consequently, I've tried to condense the basic essentials in this short manual to provide all the fundamentals you need to get started as a beekeeper, so that you can begin to build a thriving bee farm.

As you pursue the art and science of beekeeping, may you draw nearer to the Creator in whose likeness you have been created, as you learn more about His creation that is sometimes known as the "little book" that reveals His glory.

"The heavens recount the glory of God and from the works of His hand the atmospheric plating tells." Psalm 19:1 (Author's direct translation).

# References

Root,  A.I., Root, E. R., *"ABC and XYZ of Bee Culture"*, 31st Edition,  A. I. Root Bee Company, 1959.

Root, A.I., Root, E. R., *"The ABC and XYZ of Bee Culture"*, 41st Edition,  A. I. Root Bee Company, 2007.

Townsley, Cecil, *Starting Right with Bees*, 15th Edition, A. I. Root, 1970.

Conrad, Ross, *Natural Beekeeping: Organic Approaches to Modern Apiculture*, Chelsea Green Publishing, 2007.

Graham, Joe M., *The Hive and the Honey Bee*, 9th Printing, Dadant & Sons, Inc., 2010.

Laidlaw, Harry Jr., *Contemporary Queen Rearing*, 1st Edition, Dadant & Sons, Inc., 1979.

Connor, Lawrence J., *Queen Rearing Essentials*, 1st Edition, Wicwas Press, 2009.

Y. P. Chen, J S. Pettis, M. Corona, W.P. Chen, et al., *Israeli Acute Paralysis Virus: Epidemiology, Pathogenesis, and Implication for Honey Bee Health*, PLoS Pathog, Journal, 2014.

Caron, Dewey M. et al., *Tools for Varroa Management*, 1st Edition, Honey Bee Health Coalition, Online PDF, 2015.

Kains, Maurice G., *Five Acres and Independence*, BN Publishing, 2008.

# APPENDICES

**Appendix A**          PLBF Hive Stand Plans

**Appendix B**          PLBF Pollen Patty Recipe

**Appendix C**          PLBF Candy Board Recipe & Plans

**Appendix D**          PLBF Trap-Out Cone Plans


## Directions for Blowing up Plans on Copying Machine

Place desired page in proper corner of copying machine, oriented so that portrait direction of page is aligned with proper direction of paper.  For best results, choose 11"x 17" as print out size.  Choose proper "zoom to size of paper" feature of copier until page fully covers the printed copy.

<u>Cone Trap Plan Directions</u>:  For copying cone trap plans, adjust zoom until final print out distance showing 8 inches, is approximately  8 inches on 11" x 17" paper.  Larger cones can be constructed using larger print out paper for pattern.  After printing, place screen over cone pattern, and use permanent marker to draw cut-out lines for construction of cone.  Once cone screen is cut out, staple or wire long edges of cone together to form cone, then bend staple tabs along dashed lines to provide a base that can be stapled, taped or nailed to the hive entrance for trap out.  The exit hole at the tip of the cone needs to be approximately 3/8" to allow bees to easily exit.  A 3/8" diameter pen can be used to help form this opening. 8 x 8 wire mesh is the optimum screen material, but common metal door screen material can be used. Metallic screen is preferred, since it provides an appropriate stiffness.

# APPENDIX A

## Hive Stand Plans

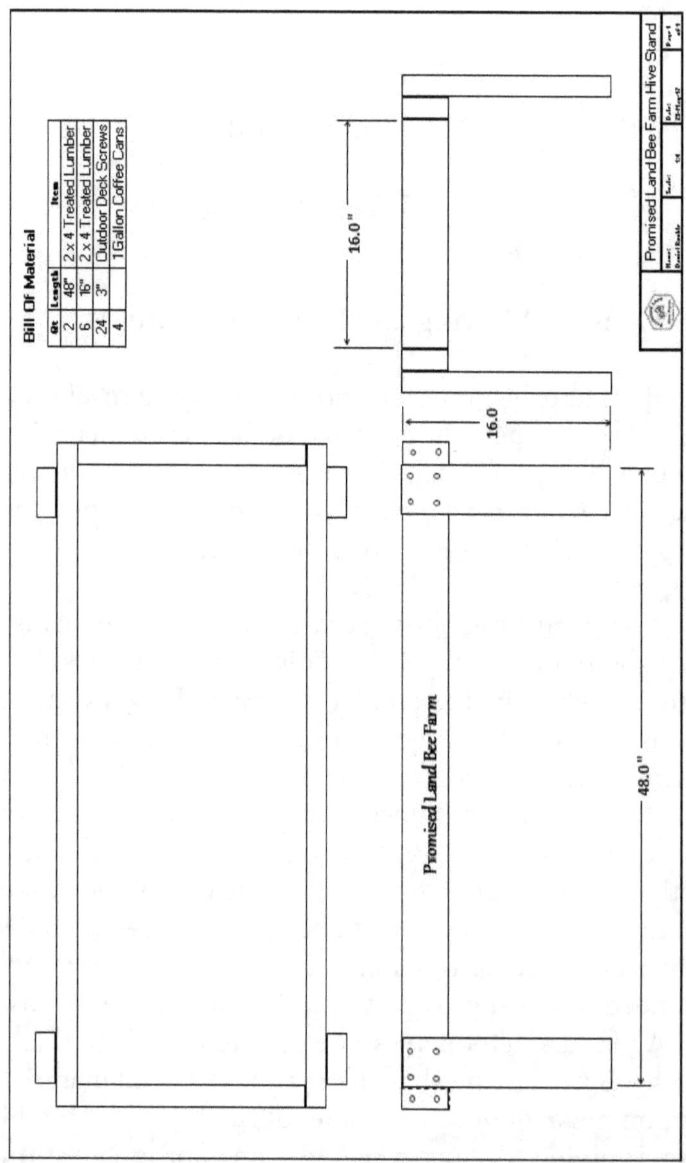

# APPENDIX B

**Promised Land Bee Farm Pollen Pattie Recipe**

**Dry Ingredients – Flour/Yeast**

| | |
|---|---|
| 1 Cup | Fat Free Soy Flour |
| ½ Cup | Brewer's Yeast |

**Wet Ingredients – Sugar Syrup**

| | |
|---|---|
| 1 Cup | Granulated Refined Sugar |
| ½ Cup | Warm Water |
| ½ Tsp | Pro Health – Feed Stimulant (w/ Essential Oils) |
| 1 Tsp | Olive Oil |
| 3 Tbsp | Lecithin |

**Directions:**

First, mix wet ingredients together in measuring bowl until sugar and other ingredients are dissolved.  Next, mix dry ingredients together in glass or stainless steel mixing bowl. After dry ingredients are mixed, slowly add Sugar Syrup mixture until mixture becomes a cookie dough consistency. Allow mixture to sit for 5 minutes for ingredients to absorb.

Mix dough with hands and form ½ pound hamburger size patties, or round balls, which are then placed on wax paper. Use 3 inch by 8 inch rectangles of wax paper to sandwich balls or patties between.  Then, use a rolling pin to roll out the sandwiched patties in a rectangular or oblong shape that is approximately ¼ in thick.

These patties can then be placed upon the top bars of the frames over the winter cluster.  Be sure to cut slits on the down facing wax paper at the time of placement, so that bees can more easily access the patties. Some people remove the bottom wax paper.  (Wax paper helps keep the patties from drying out while bees feed over time.)

# APPENDIX C

## Promised Land Bee Farm Candy Board –Recipe

To prepare the "candy" for the candy board, make sure to have your constructed candy board and the following ingredients ready to cook and assemble with the candy board.

**Ingredients/Parts**

5 lb Bag of Refined White Sugar
2 Cups of Water
Confectioner's Thermometer
Constructed Candy board

Place the 2 cups of water in a fairly large stainless steel pot. Use at least a 16 cup, or 1 gallon pot for the mixing of the 5 lbs of sugar and the 2 cups of water.  Heat the water over medium heat, and then add the 5 lbs of sugar, stirring the mixture with a spoon as it gradually heats up to the required 248 F candy making temperature.  After the candy has reached its 248F temperature, remove the pan from the heat for a couple of minutes before pouring into the candy board frame.

<u>CAUTION</u>:  Serious burns can occur from hot liquefied hot sugar solution spills.  Make certain the candy board frame is set on a level secure surface before pouring, and use caution while pouring.

Carefully pour the hot sugary candy mixture into the candy board, until the level of candy comes up close to the top of the inner rim.  Allow candy board to cool until board and candy reaches room temperature.

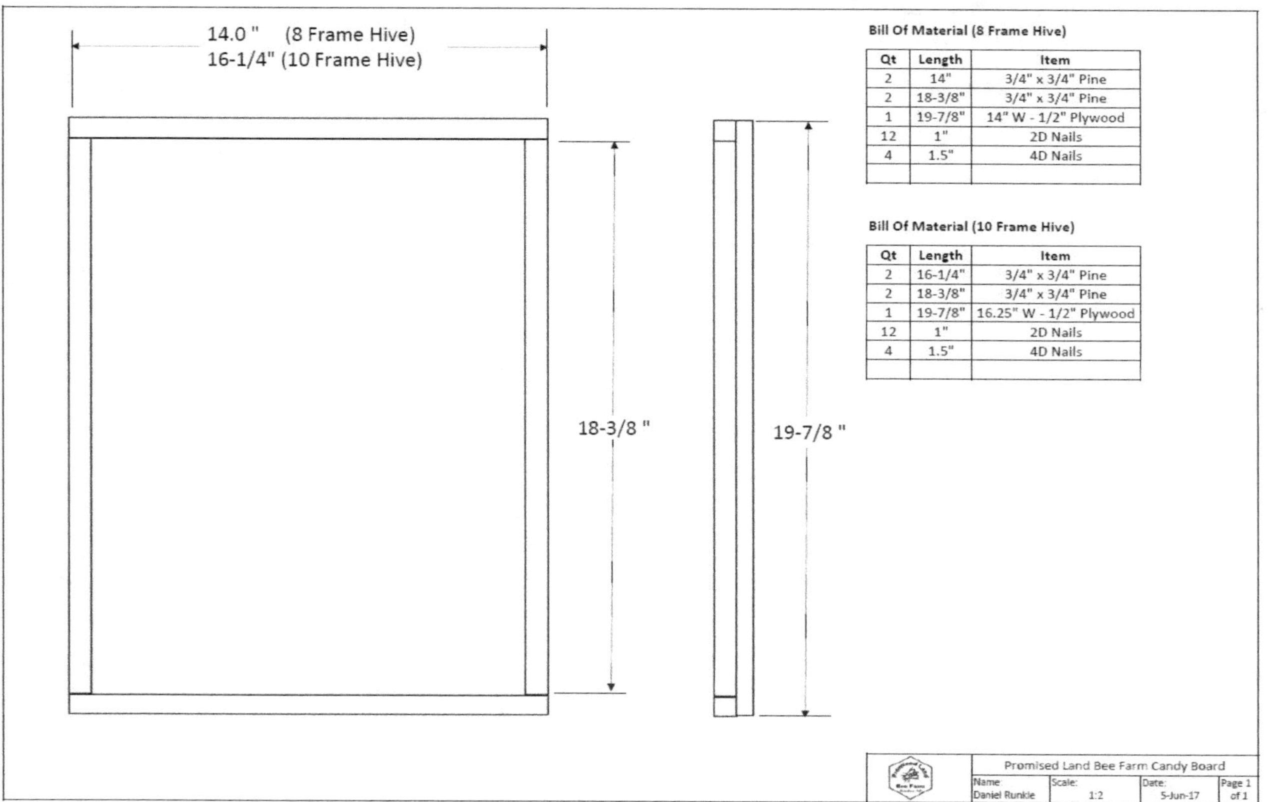



**Bill Of Material (8 Frame Hive)**

| Qt | Length | Item |
|---|---|---|
| 2 | 14" | 3/4" x 3/4" Pine |
| 2 | 18-3/8" | 3/4" x 3/4" Pine |
| 1 | 19-7/8" | 14" W - 1/2" Plywood |
| 12 | 1" | 2D Nails |
| 4 | 1.5" | 4D Nails |
|  |  |  |

**Bill Of Material (10 Frame Hive)**

| Qt | Length | Item |
|---|---|---|
| 2 | 16-1/4" | 3/4" x 3/4" Pine |
| 2 | 18-3/8" | 3/4" x 3/4" Pine |
| 1 | 19-7/8" | 16.25" W - 1/2" Plywood |
| 12 | 1" | 2D Nails |
| 4 | 1.5" | 4D Nails |
|  |  |  |

# APPENDIX D
## Promised Land Bee Farm Trap-Out Cone Plans

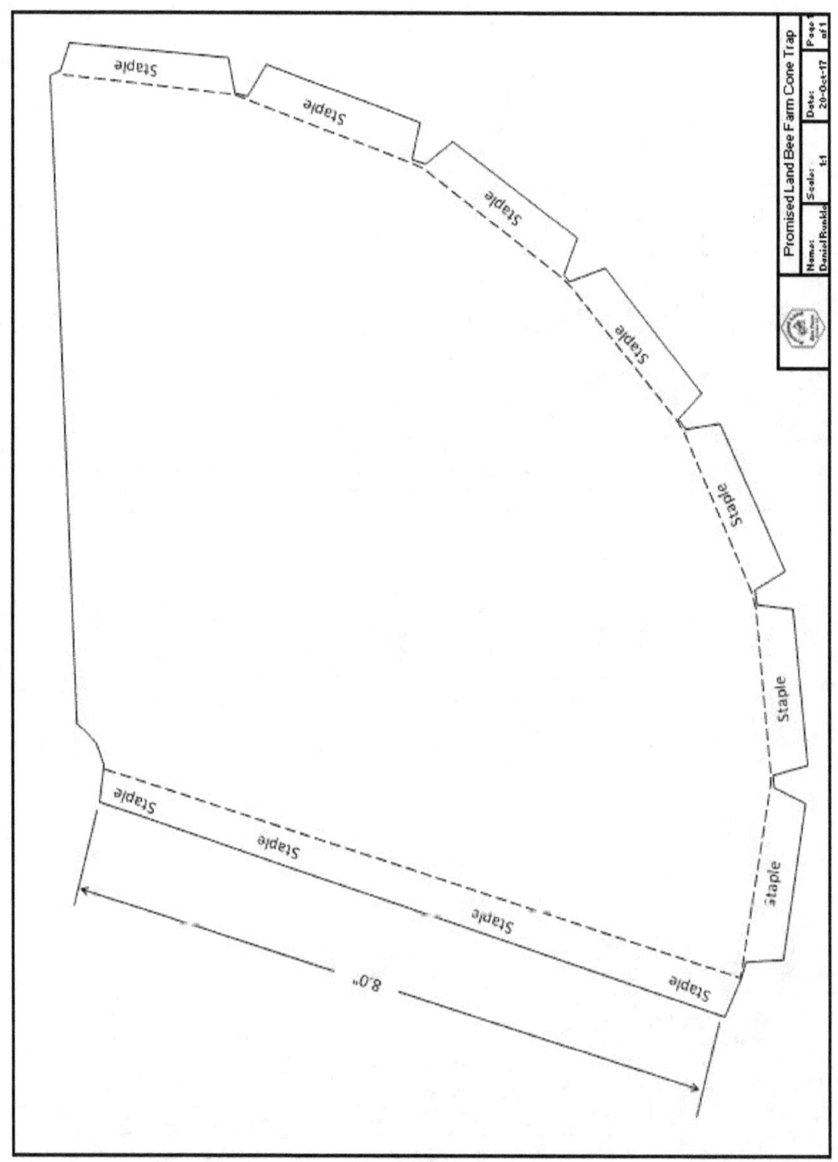

# Index